More praise for
Coping with the Stressed-Out People in Your Life

"Dealing with your own stress without coping with the stressed-out people in your life is like clapping with one hand. Now, authors Nathan and Stuart have given us this helping hand. Their method is effective, easy to remember, and should become an important life skill for everyone who does not live on a desert island."

—Elaine Fantle Shimberg,
author of *Gifts of Time*
and *Strokes: What Families Should Know*

"If you don't usually handle obnoxious, stressed-out people by giving them support, you have to read this book. It will make your life considerably easier!"

—Albert J. Bernstein, Ph.D.,
author of *Sacred Bull* and *Dinosaur Brains*

"We have many books about how to deal with our own stress and on how, as professionals, to help patients deal with stress, but this is the only one that I have seen designed for helping all of us help each other. That we should care for each other is a basic teaching of nearly all world philosophies, but this book tells us *how*."

—Thomas L. Leaman, M.D.,
Professor Emeritus, Family and Community
Medicine, Penn State College of Medicine

"There is much written on coping with your own stress, and now we have something to help when those we care about are feeling stress. *Coping with Stressed-Out People in Your Life* is a wonderful book for people in all walks of life."

—Dorothy Firman,
coauthor of *Daughters and Mothers,
Healing the Relationship*; Director,
Synthesis Center, Amherst, Massachusetts

"*Coping with Stressed-Out People in Your Life* is must reading for anyone other than hermits! Virtually all of us live life at a frantic pace beset with stresses and strains that, if they don't affect us personally, can certainly affect those around us. Improving our ability to deal with these problems improves our own quality of life and can be a god-send to those with whom we come in contact."

—Joseph A. Lieberman, III, M.D., M.P.H.,
Chairman, Department of Family and
Community Medicine, Wilmington Hospital

Coping with the Stressed-Out People in Your Life

RONALD G. NATHAN, Ph.D.,
and MARIAN R. STUART, Ph.D.

BALLANTINE BOOKS
· *New York*

All rights reserved under International and Pan-American Copyright Conventions. Published in the United States by Ballantine Books, a division of Random House, Inc., New York, and simultaneously in Canada by Random House of Canada Limited, Toronto.

Grateful acknowledgment is made to Robert J. Franke for permission to reprint lines from the song "Bob Franke's Dream Come True," copyright © 1982 by Robert J. Franke.

Library of Congress Catalog Card Number: 94-94356
ISBN: 0-345-38186-6

Cover design by Susan Grube

Manufactured in the United States of America
First Edition: November 1994
10 9 8 7 6 5 4 3 2 1

*To our parents
and our children
who have been our teachers*

CONTENTS

ACKNOWLEDGMENTS

We wish to acknowledge our equal contributions to the ideas in this book and to state that we placed our names alphabetically only by convention.

Special thanks go to John Ware, our agent and friend, who skillfully redirected a flawed proposal, encouraged us to be true to ourselves, and stood by us when *we* were all stressed out. We also appreciate deeply Cheryl Woodruff, our dedicated, hands-on editor, who listened to us, contributed creatively, and stretched us to go beyond our limits.

We wish to thank Alice Fruehan, M.D., who supported us in many ways and introduced us two years ago by lending R.N. a tape of one of M.S.'s workshops that Dr. Fruehan attended. Anthony Greenberg, M.D., helped us stay connected by setting up our modem, and Marcia Neu equipped us with a temporary computer at an STFM meeting.

Our thanks go to everyone who cheered us on, gave us ideas, or read early drafts, including especially Gene Bont, M.D.; Phyllis Bont, R.N., F.N.P.; Jean Johnson; Robert Like, M.D.; Joseph Lieberman, III, M.D.; Isabel Mitnick, R.N.; Neil Mitnick, D.O.; Jane Matey; Hinda Nathan; Kurt Nathan, Ph.D.; Joanne Nanos, M.S., Ed.S.; Evelynn Ryan; Reverend Fred Shilling; Mary Smith, M.S.W., Ph.D.; Andrew Sommers, L.L.D.; David Swee, M.D.; Alfred Tallia, M.D., M.P.H.; Judy Williams; and many other colleagues.

Friends and family bear a special burden when authors give birth to a book. We want to thank all of our friends, but both of us want to give thanks to our family members by name for all that they have given us.

Jennifer Nathan and William Nathan hugged their busy father daily; his sisters, Vivian Campbell and Susan Nathan, Ph.D., spoke to his needs through generous telephone support; and finally, his loving parents, Hinda Nathan and Kurt Nathan, Ph.D., encouraged him in many special ways.

We would like to thank Peter Stuart, Laurie Stuart, Robert Stuart, and Sarah Clark Stuart, who never lost faith in their mom. Also Irene and Jop Van Overveen, who provide warm, ongoing support across a continent. And finally, Margot Alexander, in the hope that this book, coauthored by her daughter, will bring her pleasure.

Finally, we would like to give thanks for everyone who came into our lives to teach us what we can now share with you.

Coping with the Stressed-Out People in Your Life

Introduction

"In order to find peace, we must respond peacefully."
—AUTHOR UNKNOWN

Turning on the news or opening a daily paper would convince anyone that we live in a century of stress. The lead stories affect us all—violent crime, economic downturns, tax hikes, international terrorism, and natural disasters. The inside pages headline personal crises—BOY DROWNS, FIRE KILLS FAMILY OF FOUR, and WORKERS FACE MORE LAYOFFS. In addition we are increasingly aware of global dangers—ozone depletion, overpopulation, and environmental destruction.

At work we face increasing pressure to do more and more, in less and less time, with fewer and fewer resources. These conditions breed tension and friction between co-workers, many of whom are also struggling with personal crises. Yet productivity requires teamwork. As competition intensifies, we cannot survive, much less succeed, unless everyone pulls together.

At home the impact of social change on our most intimate

3

relationships is also inescapable. Empty nests have become crowded and angry nests. Members of a sandwich generation now stretch and strain to care for aging parents and demanding children. Everyone is stressed-out.

Stress and Relationships

Stress is our built-in, fight-or-flight-or-freeze response to anything we perceive as dangerous, demanding, or demoralizing. It was adaptive for the cave dweller, whose defense, escape, or hiding from wild animals preserved human life. In this very basic way, one could argue, stress also preserved the cave dweller's relationships.

Today this fight-or-flight-or-freeze response is triggered in excess, not by saber-toothed tigers but by everything we see as threatening. The association between stress and illness is well known. Unfortunately until now we have not paid sufficient attention to the effects of the stress response on our relationships.

When people are ready to fight, their anger threatens us. When they flee, their withdrawal frustrates us. When they freeze, their immobility blocks our interactions. All three *F* responses jeopardize our relationships.

People under stress fight us, not with stones, spears, and clubs but with attacks of angry criticism, barbed sarcasm, and unreasonable demands.

Have you ever been caught off guard by anger that seemed completely out of proportion to what was going on? Been badgered by unrealistic demands for work that should take a month rather than a week or a day? Ever felt like you've been a dartboard for criticism from a boss, a parent, or a child? Doesn't it feel, sometimes, as if everyone is asking for a fight?

On the other hand, people in flight disappear either during or after a confrontation. Some people take flight immediately. Others avoid us later and just can't be reached. They might as well have left the planet. Our telephone calls are never returned.

We have added "freeze" as a third part of the stress response. Like the deer blinded by oncoming headlights, some people are immobilized by a crisis. They suffer from an inability to respond. They are not purposefully withdrawing. Their systems simply shut down.

When people are physically present but seem cold and distant, it is difficult to tell whether they are withdrawing or freezing. Sometimes freezing takes the form of numbing out. Needing to look good, even to themselves, some people numb out and deny feeling overwhelmed. They seem to hide behind soundproof walls while mumbling polite refrains of "I'm fine; I'm fine; I'm just fine."

In addition it's not always fight-*or*-flight-*or*-freeze. Many times we are confronted by a combination of responses, sometimes even a triple threat. These may be difficult to recognize because they often involve that sugar-coated hostility of unyielding, passive-aggressive behavior. Somehow we know we've been had, but we just can't prove it. Or the combination may be more obvious, like the sarcastic remarks thrown at us by someone going out the door. Any of these responses by stressed-out people can be disruptive and upsetting.

We're All in This Together

"Sometimes I get so frustrated," admitted a worried-looking woman during one of our workshops, "I wonder why God doesn't just get rid of the people who irritate us." She then added, half jokingly, "Doesn't he care?" Several other people laughed and confessed to sometimes wondering the same thing.

The question raises some rather profound issues. Many people believe that we attract certain people into our lives to help us face specific problems within ourselves. These relationships-create opportunities for us to learn something that we need to learn. It may be useful to look at difficult situations in this way.

In any case, another woman came up with a simple reply: "If God got rid of everybody who irritated anybody, nobody would be left!"

When people go beyond irritating us and begin fighting, fleeing, or freezing, we may feel attacked, abandoned, or aggravated. Their stress becomes our stress. We lose our sense of control. We feel caught in the middle of a dangerous and sometimes infuriating chain reaction. It can make us want to retaliate, withdraw, or shut down ourselves. When we are forced into a corner, we may feel threatened and decide that the best defense is an all-out attack.

Each of us wants to live in a warm and safe environment, a peaceful world that supports and nurtures us. Many times the only way to achieve this for ourselves is to create it for others. By responding to attacks from people around us with greater composure and understanding, we create healthier climates at home and at work. Until then, whether a given stress reaction begins in the form of fight, flight, freeze, or any combination of the three Fs, it undermines not only our physical and mental health but also our work productivity and interpersonal security.

Stress Management: Then and Now

We have conducted stress management workshops since the late 1970s. The enthusiastic and grateful reports of improved health and well-being have been most rewarding to us. Each year, however, more and more participants have asked for help with all the stressed-out people in their lives. Not only have these requests increased, but they are different now and require new responses.

When we started presenting stress management workshops, people would occasionally ask us how to deal with an ornery spouse or boss. They would usually explain that the person was clearly under stress but refused to change or to get help. At first we focused on ways people could protect and take care of themselves, particularly when criticized. We helped them learn how to apply relaxation techniques, make attitudinal adjustments, and express themselves assertively in these situations.

But the number of people asking how to relate to stressed-out people seemed to multiply. Many times assertiveness training didn't work. We were told that even the best "I feel" messages were heard as accusations by many people under stress. So those who asked for ways to relate wanted more and better answers.

Many folks were well on the way to solving their own problems with stress but wanted to know how to cope with the people around them. As one young woman said, "I've got my stress under control, but it's my husband's stress, my boss's stress, my secretary's stress, my neighbor's stress, my customer's stress, and my mother's stress that bother me." That summed it up.

In stressful situations, people who had completed our training were able to change their inner experience and stand up for their rights, but the chain reactions of stress continued to rattle them; they still didn't know what to say when others were fuming with anger, stricken by grief, or hiding behind frozen exteriors.

We found ourselves flooded with requests for techniques that would work when conflicts strained relationships at home and at work. People wanted to know how to defuse explosive anger, calm everyone down, and help everyone come together. After all, if a problem is between people, it is best to look interpersonally for solutions.

The Bigger Picture

Historically America was founded on the transcending principle of individual rights. Isolationism has been our most frequent response to international conflict. Capitalism emphasizes competition over cooperation. It is not surprising that almost all the popular stress management techniques of the past were self-help skills for personal survival and success. Now more than ever there is a growing need to focus on relationships, interdependence, and social support as buffers to stress.

Unfortunately the pace and change of modern life have undermined our sense of community. More than half of today's marriages end in divorce. Over 60 percent of children born today will spend part of their childhood in a single-parent household. Still other people are homeless. People are broke, busted, and disgusted.

Where are we, decades after President Johnson's Great Society programs? Social programs vary widely in effectiveness, and all face shrinking dollars. Government programs have not solved our social problems.

Where are we after a century of psychotherapy? Many people have been helped, but without therapeutic life experiences in a nurturing community, individual progress is difficult to sustain. Furthermore there are simply not enough mental-health counselors to meet these needs.

Adding up the number of social workers, guidance counselors, psychologists, psychiatric nurses, psychiatrists, and clergy in 1990, we found roughly 1.2 million potential counselors. Even if we assume that all of them, including the clergy, were providing counseling on a full-time basis, there would only be one counselor for every 207 people in the United States. On the other hand if we add up the number of people in military, police, and security jobs, we find three times the number of counselors, one for every sixty-nine people.

As social programs falter because of funding or design, and as the pressures of living intensify, fewer people can afford the time or money for psychotherapy. We've drifted along and relied on obsolete skills for far too long. We need to learn new, creative ways to communicate. Now is the time for ordinary people to reach out and help one another.

Most wars are terrifying escalations on an international scale of the sort of chain reactions triggered by stressed-out people. If peace is ever to be brought to the world, we must bring it first to our families, friends, co-workers, and communities. Ultimately when enough of us respond peacefully, we will create a more peaceful world. As ordinary individuals, we can promote peace by learning to de-escalate retaliatory reactions to the stressed-out people in our lives.

These larger needs and directions are related to the changing questions we kept hearing in our workshops. New questions call for new answers. As practicing psychologists and educators, we were excited by the potential for strengthening social networks by empowering ordinary people as natural helpers.

The Challenge

As we emphasize in our workshops, not all stress is bad. In addition to its survival benefits when we face physically dangerous situations, it gives us our energy and enthusiasm for living and for trying new things. Of course too much stress can lead to distress.

In designing a new training program, however, we knew that most people would be coming to us under considerable stress and that some would clearly be in distress. This could interfere with their ability to learn and remember ways of coping with others under stress. After all, if you can't learn it or remember it, you can't use it.

So we needed to find or create very practical solutions that would be simple to learn, easy to remember, and rewarding to use. We created two major methods.

The first is a powerful way to connect with stressed-out people by understanding and getting beyond the smoke screens of attack, retreat, or numbing out. The second is an equally powerful way to offer emotional first aid to people under stress.

To make these methods useful, at critical moments when

people encounter others under stress, we needed to find ways to help learners immediately recall the steps in each approach.

To help people remember and use the first method, we developed a series of disarming and peaceful "agree-or-set-free" responses to the disruptive and dangerous fight, flight, or freeze responses of stress. For the second method we created an acronym, a word whose letters trigger a sequence of special questions and comments that provide powerful emotional support. This is H.E.L.P.

We then discovered that people could use H.E.L.P. when they were stressed out themselves. Using the method to relieve their own stress gave them valuable practice, increased their confidence, and enabled them to give H.E.L.P. more effectively to others.

Simple but Flexible

We also recognized that people's styles and situations vary widely and might call for different levels of intimacy. First of all, men and women relate differently to people under stress. As Deborah Tannen documented in *You Just Don't Understand* (Ballantine, 1991), men typically respond to other people's problems with solutions. In general, they attend to issues of status, independence, and competency. Women typically respond to other people's problems with sympathy and relate their own experiences in similar situations. In general, they attend to issues of confirmation, dependence, and connectedness.

There are hazards in both of these approaches. When men try to solve another person's problems, they undermine that person's feeling of competency. When women share their own struggles, they take attention away from the other person's experiences and leave them feeling disconnected.

Are there communication patterns that fulfill the best intentions of both men and women? We believe that by combining H.E.L.P. with Support, a special framework is created that can

help everyone, male or female, feel more competent and connected.

Secondly, as our editor has pointed out, many men might
have great difficulty asking people, particularly at work, how
they *feel* about a personal crisis. The current men's literature
has eloquently described how lonely and empty the male experience can be. This is not surprising, given that our culture
generally discourages men from connecting on an emotional
level.

Even for women, asking about feelings might create problems in otherwise formal relationships. Women might inappro-
priately share their experiences when they are at a loss for an
otherwise helpful response.

One of the authors (Marian Stuart, Ph.D.) first organized
some of these techniques into an acronym to help family doctors communicate more effectively with their patients. Dr. Stuart's book about this approach, *The Fifteen Minute Hour*, and
her workshops have made it the leading communication technique in primary-care medicine. Toward the end of most workshops, doctors generally start discussing how they plan to use
the technique with their spouses, children, and office staff, as
well as with their patients.

H.E.L.P. and Support offers enough flexibility to address an
even wider range of needs and comfort zones. Once learned,
it can easily be modified to apply in almost any situation and
relationship.

Why do we say "almost"? Because people and relationships
involving long-standing personality problems must be ap-
proached cautiously and with realistic expectations. In addition, our techniques are not designed to help you cope with
psychotics, substance abusers, or the seriously disturbed.
While they may make a small difference, they are far more
helpful with the other stressed-out people in your life.

If you've come to this book to help a specific person who is
feeling overwhelmed with grief, shock, guilt, disappointment,
fear, or any other emotion, and his or her interaction with you

is completely free of anger, you may be able to go directly to the H.E.L.P. and Support techniques in Chapter 6 and beyond. If, however, you feel under attack of any kind, we strongly recommend protecting yourself with disarming techniques from Chapters 2 and 3 before you try to help the other person.

The Results

We have taught our new techniques to a large number of people attending our workshops. They learn the techniques quickly and use them effectively to make interacting with stressed-out people less exhausting and more fulfilling.

People from all walks of life are surprised how much they help. Teachers cope more easily with stressed-out students and parents. CEOs improve their interactions with high-powered board members. Salespeople deal more competently with stressed-out customers. And bankers, bartenders, lawyers, taxi drivers, realtors, beauticians, and accountants are able to calm stressed clients.

By using the techniques, people learn important things about themselves and others. All these competencies and connections reduce their stress and strengthen their relationships.

Many folks also report an increased level of self-confidence and self-esteem. When under stress they find themselves running through H.E.L.P. to quickly sort out their own feelings and options. By recognizing and responding to stressful chain reactions, they regain control, handle anger, avoid withdrawal, learn from complaints, and reach workable solutions. As a result they are able to go from fight-or-flight-or-freeze to flow.

In this way they are not only more productive but they have won new respect from their bosses, colleagues, friends, and loved ones. Moreover they enjoy the immense rewards of reaching out and helping others.

An Invitation

Come with us now as we look at the stress of high-speed living and how it distorts relationships. Join with us as we share our methods, step by step, and show you how to H.E.L.P. yourself before you H.E.L.P. others. Then once you've had some practice, we'll expand the model and introduce you to even more H.E.A.L.T.H.Y. ways to be in the world.

We hope the journey through this book will help you to connect with us and discover what wonderful things you can do for yourself and your relationships.

PART I

COPING WITH PEOPLE ON TILT

1

People
and Relationships on Tilt

"These are the times that try men's souls."
—THOMAS PAINE

For three years Larry has enjoyed learning about the publishing world as Susan's editorial assistant at a regional magazine. Today, it's been a difficult morning. The aging copier is broken and the repairman has not arrived as promised. Also, Susan seems preoccupied. Larry has come to expect that, but only around the deadline for each issue.

Unexpectedly Susan storms out of her office yelling, "Why haven't you sent Dan a copy of the revisions? Don't you know that he's going on vacation and needs to approve it by tomorrow? Do I have to check up on every detail around here?"

As Larry tells himself that everyone in the office is looking up and waiting for his response, he feels his face getting red.

Jenny is sixteen and a half. A quiet girl who likes to read, Jenny has recently started to talk back to her parents at every opportunity. Her mother, Judy, wants to find out what's going on with Jenny but is having a hard time dealing with her own anger. After all, Jenny hasn't made her bed or picked up her room in weeks. More important Judy wonders and worries, *Could Jenny be involved in something serious?*

Judy discussed the situation with her husband, John, but he was of no help. First he tried to fix the situation by yelling at Jenny to clean up her room. When that didn't work, and Jenny snapped back, "You can't make me," he stormed out of the house. When he returned, he was angry at Judy and refused to discuss it any further. Now Judy is frantic. She knows she needs to do something, but doesn't know what.

Bill hasn't seen Joe around the office for a few weeks, so when he sees him in the cafeteria, he takes his coffee and heads in his direction. Joe looks terrible. There are dark circles under his eyes, and his clothes are wrinkled.

As Bill comes closer, Joe motions for him to sit down. Bill needs to get back to some important paperwork and wonders how he can escape without hurting Joe's feelings. Obviously his friend is in deep trouble, but Bill knows he really doesn't have the time to get involved in whatever is bringing Joe down.

Have you ever found yourself at a loss for words in the face of another person's grief or anger? Felt helpless when someone became withdrawn after losing a job or a promotion? Have you ever wanted to reach out to a friend going through a divorce, but feared getting into the middle of an emotional hurricane?

Do you sometimes get frustrated trying to interact with people in the midst of everyday hassles?

Are there times when everyone around you seems to be preoccupied by impossible deadlines, disabled cars, and uncontrollable kids? Do you find yourself bruised by criticism from people under stress?

If you answered yes to any of these questions, you are probably alive. Life can sometimes be bruising, even brutal. And we live with people who are often in pain.

The Crisis of Crises

A crisis is an emotionally significant event, a turning point, often involving a radical change in status. At a time when the rate of change in our culture is accelerating faster than ever before in history, more people are facing more turning points than ever before. We change jobs, cities, even spouses more rapidly now than in the past. It is important to remember that all change is demanding and thus inherently stressful.

Then there are the mini-crises of modern life—the bounced check, the stolen wallet, the late report, the bent fender, the lost letter, the canceled flight. Need we go on?

At times these crises are like kernels of corn in a popcorn machine—we never know when or where the next one will pop or burn.

Stress and Crises Put People on Tilt

Daily stress and crises upset our equilibrium. It's as if we are on "tilt." When our lives go off balance and we feel like we are leaning precariously over a cliff, we're on tilt.

Anytime we feel out of control, off center, and vulnerable, we're on tilt. Tilt is our response to stress when we become aware that we are just not functioning competently. We over-react and sometimes become depressed. We "awfulize," personalize, and "catastrophize."

People on tilt misjudge other people and events. They don't solve problems well. They suffer from narrowed vision and always figure the light at the end of the tunnel is an oncoming train. People on tilt tend to lash out at others. Trying to regain their balance, they often knock other people down. So stress and crises put both people and relationships on tilt.

The Combat Zone

We spend much of our daily lives interacting with pressured people at work, distressed friends at leisure, and upset family members at home. People under stress are prepared for fight-flight-or-freeze. They often express their anger explosively through criticism or flee the scene. Others just freeze and withdraw into painful shells. It is hard to tell what goes on under their cold exteriors.

All too often stress begets stress. When others are on tilt, we go on tilt. Stress and tilt are contagious. Everyone's stress builds until we all feel like we are in a combat zone. We may not even know where our stress is coming from, but we fear the repercussions of an eerie silence and prepare for the next grenade.

The Domino Effect

It is clear that not everyone under stress goes on tilt in the same way. When people are under stress, it's as important to be prepared for the freeze as the fight or flight in the fight-or-flight-or-freeze response. Some people angrily criticize those around them. Some remove themselves from the action. Others become cold and aloof. Attack, withdrawal, and indifference may each have a different effect on us and may call for different responses, but they are all reactions to threat or lack of control. Any of them can disrupt our equilibrium.

Let's put this into a new perspective by looking at the similarities between dominoes and people. We are going to stretch the analogy pretty thin, but if you go along with us, all the pieces will fall into place.

Dominoes and People Go on Tilt

Have you ever played dominoes? The small black, rectangular playing pieces are marked into halves, and each half has up to six white dots. In the game, players take turns laying dominoes down by finding ones with matching patterns. During the game the dominoes are flat on the table, well supported and very stable. The patterns match one with another, very much the way people with common interests connect with each other. The game is very simple, predictable, and sometimes even boring.

If you don't know the game or don't enjoy it, you might play with the pieces in another way. Maybe you've played with a domino by standing it up on its shortest side. Just as life pulls us up short during crises, a domino in this position is not very stable. It can easily go on tilt.

If you stand the dominoes up, one next to the other, like people in a line, and you put one of them on tilt, you can start a chain reaction. The dominoes lean and fall one onto the next. If the chain is long, it's like a major news story that puts everyone on tilt. If the chain is short, or there is enough distance between groups of dominoes, the effect is more like a personal crisis. It affects only the few dominoes around it.

When people are in pain and go on tilt by withdrawing, we may need to catch them as they fall backward. If they fall away from us when they are essential at work or home, we may need to reengage them. If they push hard and angrily to get away from us or pull back abruptly to suck us into a frightening vacuum, we may need to cope with their hostility.

When people go on tilt and fall forward, they may come down hard on us with angry criticism or brutal sarcasm. Sometimes they don't just lean on us a little, they collide with us. Whether people fall forward or backward, if we're standing too close, we will be caught in a dangerous chain reaction of stress. People on tilt need a lot of room. We hope to teach you how to give them the physical and emotional space they need.

Angry Dominoes

Most of us don't like to be criticized. No one was ever born goof-proof and we all have to learn from our mistakes, but all too often feedback is laced with anger. And the anger has very little to do with us.

Have you ever taken a beating for something you had nothing to do with? Ever felt like someone you trusted just turned from Dr. Jekyll into Mr. Hyde? If so, you have probably experienced the domino effect.

People who are angry but afraid to strike out at a boss, teacher, police officer, or other powerful person may redirect the anger onto someone less powerful or someone closer to them. This defense mechanism is called displacement. It is played out when a father who has been taken to task at work yells at his wife, who screams at one of their children, who pulls the dog's tail. No wonder cats keep their distance and mice are always scurrying for cover.

There is another reaction with similar effects. Some people who are angry at themselves and feel they've failed may either fear the wrath of higher-ups or find fault with those they supervise. This unconscious mechanism is called projection. People can project their anger, their inadequacy, or both.

When people go on tilt, the tension level around them rises. Anyone who is close enough may also go on tilt. Tempers shorten. Fears deepen. Hopelessness spreads. Any of these stressful feelings can be displaced or projected onto other people or situations. Soon everyone is on tilt. . . . And we all fall down.

This is the domino effect of stress. It can get out of control very quickly. Each person knocks another down. Some people can wipe out several at one time. On a given day we may be standing at the crossroads of two or more falling lines of dominoes.

Too Many People on Tilt

As the population grows, particularly in the cities, crowding intensifies and multiplies these stressful contacts. In less than a lifetime, Americans over the age of sixty have seen the population of the country double. Wherever there was one, there are now two, except that the proportion of people living in cities has grown from 50 to 75 percent.

With less elbow room we all need better ways to disarm oncoming dominoes and communicate caring to those falling away from us. When we don't know how to respond peacefully and help one another, we are forced to cope with chaos.

In experiments where scientists crowded more and more rats into limited spaces, they discovered unusual reactions. Female rats neglected their young and ultimately became infertile. The males exhibited frantic activity or pathological withdrawal. The rat society degenerated and disintegrated. Has modern life become even worse than a rat race?

Whatever the answer, this is the background for all our activities and relationships. There are more and more people—people who are so often preoccupied by crises, isolated by mobility, and overwhelmed by the pace of life that interacting with them becomes increasingly difficult.

It is clear that we must all cope with stressed-out people who are on tilt. We must all cope with people in pain who collide with us or who back away from us.

If we can learn healthy ways to cope, however, our relationships do not have to be at the mercy of stress. Our crises and those of the people in our lives do not have to drain our energy. In fact, during a crisis, inner resources only *seem* depleted. In reality these resources are still intact; the crisis has simply made them temporarily inaccessible.

"Fallout"

People in crisis sometimes seem to be fumbling through a fog of what we call fallout. It's all the junk that came down on them when their world seemingly blew apart. This fallout prevents them from accessing their inner resources and interferes with virtually everything they do. And it gets in the way of almost everything you want to do with them. Their fallout becomes your fallout.

Just recognizing fallout and the varieties of tilt can help you understand and manage otherwise frustrating and confusing situations constructively.

When people are stressed-out, we don't have to react defensively and destructively. We don't have to fight or flee or freeze in turn. We can learn to interact productively by recognizing the problem, disarming the anger, and connecting in ways that uncover hidden resources.

When we do, we will overcome loneliness, both theirs and ours, empower one another, and start to create a caring community.

2

Self-protection

*"The amount of pain people inflict on others is
directly proportional to the amount they feel within."*
—AUTHOR UNKNOWN

Attacked, avoided, or frozen out by a stressed-out person,
we sense danger and thereby trigger our own stress response.
The dominoes start falling. Where there was one stressed-out
person, now there are two or more.

When Larry's editor, Susan, suddenly stormed out of her office yelling, "Why haven't you sent Dan a copy of the revisions?" and repeatedly questioned his competence, Larry felt
like striking back or finding a way to crawl under the wall-to-
wall carpeting. On the other hand, if Susan had started to
withdraw and ignore Larry or his work, he might have felt in-
sulted and then attacked or avoided her in retaliation. All too
often this leads to wasted time around the water cooler and an
escalation of the stress spiral.

When someone attacks with criticism, we may not even realize what's happened until after we leave the heat of the en-

counter or recover from the rejection. We may just feel upset and off balance because the situation got out of control.

No one likes to be criticized. Angry criticism abrasively eats away and destroys both relationships and self-esteem. Often we know that the person is displacing or projecting, but we react defensively anyway.

Criticism reminds us of bad feelings from our childhood—those feelings of incompetence when everyone seemed bigger, stronger, and wiser. So, like most people, we respond to criticism in one of the four childish ways Mary Lynne Heldmann described so well in her book, *When Words Hurt* (Ballantine, 1990).

When our parents criticized us, we learned to avoid punishment by defending what we had done, denying that we had done it, counterattacking or withdrawing. As Heldmann points out, if we defend ourselves and search for excuses, we cannot listen effectively. If we deny, we discredit the person's perceptions and undermine his or her self-esteem. If we counterattack or withdraw, we interfere with good communications and undermine our relationships. Unfortunately most of us continue to respond to criticism with one of these patterns. In so doing we promote the domino effect and build resentment.

A Contest Where Everyone Loses

Think about the last time someone angrily criticized you. Perhaps it caught you off guard. Maybe you counterattacked and tried to win. Perhaps you felt that you just couldn't let the person get away with it. You felt you had to prove yourself and you made a contest out of it by searching for a clever comeback, a perfect put-down, or a wicked wisecrack.

It's tempting, but risky. Not so much because we might fail as because such responses alienate people, and everyone loses in that kind of contest. Anger is unlikely to persuade. It's unlikely that any new and exciting solutions are found, and a lot of time and energy gets drained. Feelings fester. Unless the other person is a complete stranger that we'll never see again, we may have lost an ally and made an enemy. In addition, waiting for round two of the fight puts everyone in earshot on edge.

Do You Want to Be Right or Do You Want to Be Happy?

Another temptation is to try to figure out who's right and who's wrong. When unsure, we may even seek out a third party to act as a judge. It's a little like children who look for a parent during a squabble. In reality life is not a courtroom and there are no police officers or concerned parents around to enforce interpersonal rules. In fact it makes little difference who's right; we usually have to continue living or working with the stressed-out person.

When we are tempted to wage a war over who's right and who's wrong, we may need to ask "Do I want to be right or do I want to be happy?" Temporary feelings of strength and superiority may not be worth persistent feelings of alienation and loneliness. When we consistently win arguments by making others wrong, we also lose. We're likely to spend a lot of time alone. No one likes to be around someone who stirs up feelings of inadequacy.

Taking Things Personally

The actions of stressed-out people often have little to do with us. Our tendency to take things personally may come from a desire to be so important that people would focus all their attention on us. In that case, we could do things to put people on top of the world or on tilt. Fortunately no one's that powerful. Such beliefs are often hangovers from childhood fantasies when we thought that we were the center of the universe.

So when people's anger seems out of proportion to the situation, or their withdrawal seems designed to frustrate us, it is best to remember that both are their reactions to whatever they perceive as threatening, not necessarily reactions to us or to anything we've done.

By not trying to win, not looking for who's wrong, and not taking things personally, you can short-circuit the stress spiral or at least slow it down dramatically. When situations are observed and noted rather than interpreted or judged, things do not seem to be as much out of control.

This all sounds logical, but all too often we react automatically and without thinking. Instead of one stressed-out person, suddenly there are two. The answer lies in taking care of your stress response at the moment you sense danger so that you can act instead of overreact. In other words the first step in managing stress is to recognize that you are becoming stressed, then you can apply any number of remedies.

There is an old saying in medicine that advises doctors what to do first when they face a patient with a life-threatening condition in an emergency: "Take your own pulse!"

Slowing Your Pulse

Millions of words have been written about stress management techniques. When coping with the stressed-out people in your life, we recommend finding and using one or two rapid techniques that work for you. Whether you choose a relaxation technique, such as a cue-controlled, six-second tranquilizer, or a thought-restructuring affirmation, what you need is a quick way to steady your domino.

If you've somehow managed to avoid the barrage of self-help stress solutions or can't revive a now-rusty skill that you once knew, perhaps the easiest technique to use is deep, diaphragmatic breathing. "Diaphragmatic" means from the diaphragm muscle that tenses to pull the lungs down and to create the vacuum that sucks air into our lungs.

Why are we using such a scientific word for what babies do naturally or many adults already do when they sigh deeply?

Are we trying to confirm the definition of psychology as the science of making common sense totally unintelligible?

There are differences between sighing and breathing deeply. A sigh might nonverbally communicate contempt. In addition sighs are usually not repeated enough to be of much benefit. What we are recommending is to slow down your breathing inconspicuously by taking a series of deep, satisfying breaths. The goal is to breathe easily, fully, and deeply. This can be a healing and cleansing experience.

Who has time to breathe when under attack? We need to learn to make the time to control our breathing when under attack.

Most of us automatically breathe about fourteen times a minute from the lower chest area. Under stress we begin to breathe more rapidly and unevenly from the middle and upper chest. The more anxious we get, the faster and choppier we breathe.

When we consciously take over this process and pace our breathing, we take control and take care of ourselves. When we calm down and slow our pulse, we turn down the "settings" of many other parts of our stress response. We quiet fear reactions and are truly less "up-set."

Try thinking of deep diaphragmatic breathing as "belly breathing." We find this simpler name helps many people to remember it, smile about it, and use it, not only to get focused but to lengthen their attention span. By relaxing our bodies we can allow the attack to stimulate our minds.

So you've been confronted or confounded by a stressed-out person and you've started to compose and center yourself. Now what?

Once you've relaxed and focused yourself, we recommend remembering that the amount of pain stressed-out people give others is proportionate to their own pain. It may help to memorize the quote at the beginning of this chapter.

We also recommend assuming that the greater the stress, the greater the defensiveness, and the greater the defensiveness, the greater the need to respond carefully. These are probably the healthiest assumptions to entertain, until you have evidence to the contrary.

In addition we may want to choose to treat conflict in new ways. We may want to transform it from a win-lose battle into an opportunity to learn about the stressed-out situation or person, to try out the new skills we're learning, and to bring harmony to our relationships. Even conflict that arises from other sources of stress can clear the air and reveal things to us about which we are unaware. Without dissent we may be blind to avoidable problems and attractive solutions.

Are we asking you to just sit there and take a verbal thrashing? No. Verbal violence can and should be defused, deflected, or disarmed, as we will discuss in the next chapter. There are differences between healthy disagreements, stressful reactions, and destructive assaults. Unlike the aggressors in abusive relationships, stressed-out people need support. Differences of opinion can usually be resolved temporarily or even permanently by agreeing to disagree.

We hope these suggestions and those that follow will help free us up to observe and address another's attack or avoidance with greater equanimity, patience, and strength. We hope they will also increase the odds of our finding life-enhancing and peaceful solutions.

We Often Have It Inside Out

Studies have shown that people tend to see themselves as basically good and well intentioned. They excuse their own behavior by citing the stressful circumstances they faced. When people describe the behavior of others, however, they tend to ignore the circumstances and impute personality traits to those they observe. Consider these examples: We are "overextended"; others are lazy. The needs of our families force us to earn more money and not give to charity; others are greedy and stingy. We have suffered injustices and are rightfully angry; others are hotheads who don't have a "case."

This tendency also helps to explain why we overreact to stressed-out people when they attack or avoid. We tend to exaggerate and label. It's easier to experience and justify our anger toward a mean person than toward a person in pain. It is easier to feel hurt and retaliate toward a sarcastic, rejecting snob than a person who is suffering.

Back to Larry and Susan

Let's assume Larry recognized that the situation with his editor is out of control. He's avoided taking it personally, looking for who's wrong, or labeling his boss, and he's calmed himself through rapid relaxation. Furthermore he has begun reframing the problem as an interaction between a person in pain and a second person who is choosing not to become stressed-out. Now it's time to make a major decision.

Larry can choose to let it pass, attribute it to her stress and continue removing himself emotionally from the confrontation until she calms down. He may even choose to remove himself physically from the combat zone. On the other hand, he may decide to take a small risk to eliminate the source of his stress by disarming Susan's anger. Either choice is reasonable and appropriate. The decision is likely to be based on his prior working relationship with Susan, his interpersonal skills, his time, and his energy.

In the next chapter we will introduce a dozen ways to gently disarm stressed-out people who are attacking you.

3

Disarming Others

Is it enough to recognize the disruptive responses of stressed-out people, understand them as proportionate to their pain, and find ways to maintain our own balance? Yes, it is in many situations. But we may need and want to do more.

The stressed-out person may continue to attack, we may fear escalation, and we may want to restore peace to our world. How can we do this?

Aikido (pronounced "I key dough") is one of the gentle martial arts of self-defense and suggests a wonderful alternative to traditional combat. Rather than trying to overcome the attacker with a counterattack, aikido offers ways to dodge, deflect, and disarm the assault, and we can learn to do this with words.

Like judo, it is *ju* ("soft") and bans dangerous blows, but aikido adds *ai* ("coordination") and *ki* ("breath control") to the *do* ("way"). In the last chapter we introduced diaphragmatic "belly breathing" for breath control. By showing us ways to step aside, duck, and coordinate our movement in the same direction as the attacker's, verbal aikido also helps us to dance with the destructive energy and to redirect it into harmonious energy from which everyone can benefit.

Agree with Your Attacker

Earning a "black belt" in verbal aikido is surprisingly simple. The core concept is to "coordinate," or agree with, our attackers. In this way we flow with them and redirect their energy rather than wasting ours in fight-flight-or-freeze. In addition it honors the fact that most attackers are really feeling scared, incompetent, and alone. This is why agreeing is so powerful—we are not questioning their competence, but rather connecting with them in reassuring ways.

Do we dishonestly agree with everything they say? No, just some small part with which we can truly agree. Usually we only have to clear a small path in order to walk together. Herein lies the challenge, creativity, and fun. If there is nothing to agree with, we might ask for more information in order to show that we wish to find agreement.

Each of the headings below is a powerful, aikido-like phrase that can be memorized.

"You Seem Upset."

Let's return to Larry's interaction with Susan to see how this works. Susan was coming at Larry with angry criticisms. To give himself time to think and let Susan know that he is aware something is wrong, Larry might say, "You seem upset."

This phrase demonstrates that Susan has Larry's full attention and acknowledges that she feels very strongly about the issue. It also very gently confronts Susan that there may be more going on than a constructive evaluation.

If Larry said, "You are upset," Susan might feel counterattacked. She might respond, "No, I'm not," and defensively deny what Larry observed. The qualifier *seem* clarifies that it is his opinion and not a fact.

There is agreement in "You seem upset," but it is not expected to disarm, just to defuse temporarily. As one might expect, Susan's response is still full of emphasis and fight: "You bet I am."

"Could You Run That by Me More Slowly?"

Next, to lower the volume of the attack, Larry responds with a request that shows he agrees that he'd better listen or at least that he's willing to listen. Larry asks, "You said something about Dan's column. Could you run that by me more slowly?"

When someone goes on tilt, gets angry, and ventilates through criticism, he or she often does it in front of others in a loud voice. Larry's mention of the topic and request, "Could you run that by me more slowly?" communicates his interest in what Susan is saying. In addition, as Bernstein and Rozen point out in *Dinosaur Brains* (Ballantine, 1990), asking a person to say it slowly forces him to lower his volume. Have you ever tried to yell slowly?

To avoid counterattacking and fueling the fire, Larry's request must be free of anger. He uses a calm, warm voice to move the other person toward a more productive mode of relating. He also doesn't stress or emphasize any of the words. We'll be looking more at nonverbal communication in Chapter 7.

If our communications are free of anger but the person continues to yell, we may choose to step back a few feet. When asked why we did so, we can honestly answer, "So that I can hear you better."

"Let Me Make Sure I Understand ..."

After Susan has repeated her criticism more slowly and softly, Larry says, "Let me make sure I understand. You want to know why I haven't sent Dan a copy of the revisions." This restates the criticism so that they can assess the accuracy of the communication. This continues to slow the action. It gives everyone a chance to shift from stressful, emotional responses to less-impulsive, thoughtful responses.

Repeating the criticism helps Larry to communicate his interest in the problem. It also shows that he is open-minded and not defensive.

Susan might respond, "Yes, he's going on vacation and needs to approve it by tomorrow."

In some stressful situations we may know someone who tends to respond by criticizing. When we recognize the pattern, we can disarm the attack as soon as we anticipate the criticism. How? By asking for the criticism. This invites the other person to connect and feel in control.

"I'm Glad You Told Me What's on Your Mind."

Most people are uncomfortable giving criticism. Larry can alleviate Susan's guilt by saying, "I'm glad you told me what's on your mind." In so doing, Larry also reinforces an open and honest relationship without commenting on the content of her criticism. On the other hand, if Susan does not give Larry complete and constructive criticism, he knows he'll learn less. Larry may even want to follow up by asking, "Could you tell me more of what's on your mind?"

People who cannot be open with us may stockpile anger and suffer in silence. By reinforcing openness, those inclined to save up "brown stamps" are less likely to collect enough to somehow justify never speaking with us again or sabotaging us in some other way.

In order not to annoy Susan by inordinate delay and to

show that he agrees there is an issue of time here, Larry might simply add, "The copier is down, but I've called the repairman and as soon as it's fixed, I'll bring the revisions to Dan."

"What Specifically Would You Like Me to Do Now?"

If, on the other hand, Larry didn't know about the problem or didn't have a plan, he might disarm Susan by saying, "What specifically would you like me to do now?"

This is an important request. It would continue to shift the interaction from emotional generalizations to thoughtful specifics. If there is nothing specific to be done, Susan might have admitted that the criticism was purely a way of ventilating feelings that were unrelated to his actions.

If Susan could specify the things she wanted done, it would allow Larry to comply, negotiate, or refuse each request. It also moves Susan away from just identifying the problem toward working with Larry to find solutions. Sometimes the request is surprisingly simple and immediately doable.

"I'll Plan to _____ in the Future."

Let's say Susan asks Larry to pay more attention to details. If he felt the change was reasonable, he could reply, "I'll plan to pay more attention to details in the future." In this way he would show Susan that he is willing to change.

If Larry did not want to comply with a change Susan requested, he could say, "I'll plan to think about that." This would buy him some time so that he could explain his decision when she is no longer angry. Larry could also be more specific and say, "It sounds like that's important to you. Can we set up a meeting to talk about it next week?"

By then Susan could calmly consider the reasons for Larry's decision.

"You Seemed Really Upset, Is There Anything Else Bothering You?"

Finally, now that Larry has disarmed the attack, he may choose to connect further by asking, "You seemed really upset, is there anything else bothering you?" This would give Susan an opening to tell Larry about other concerns. It can elicit hidden problems with his work or in his relationships. It also leads into opportunities to apply some of the helping and supporting techniques discussed in later chapters.

"I Really Feel Bad That You Think _____."

If Susan had launched an even more blatant and bullying attack, she might have said, "If you really cared about this magazine, you wouldn't let so many details slide." This kind of attack includes two parts.

According to linguist Suzette Haden Elgin, Ph.D., the first part is a presupposition ("Larry doesn't care about the magazine") and the second is the bait ("You let details slide"). Most people take the bait and respond defensively. After all, in Larry's job as an assistant, details make up most of his duties.

The best way for Larry to disarm this attack is to ignore the bait and tell Susan that he really feels bad that she thinks he doesn't care about the magazine. There is an important but subtle message here. Without having to say it, he communicates that he not only cares about the magazine but he cares about what Susan thinks.

"I Absolutely Agree."

Another variation on this might be "If a person really cared about this magazine, they'd be careful about details." A great way to dance with this supposedly hypothetical case is to agree completely, by saying, "I absolutely agree that details can be very important." This gently but firmly forces the attacker to be more specific.

Other variants might be "Even a man should be able to keep track of details." Larry could agree and then express his surprise or disappointment that Susan believes women are more competent than men. Still another variant might be "Even you, Larry, should be able to keep track of details." Here Larry could respond, "I agree. I'm sorry you don't believe that I'm capable." Given a reasonably good prior relationship, Susan can be expected to respond with some variation of "Of course you're capable. Now please take care of it."

"Is There Anything Else You'd Like to Tell Me?"

If the angry attacker seems to be ignoring or bulldozing over our gentle maneuvers, we can wait silently and breathe deeply until we can ask, "Is there anything else you'd like to tell me?" The silence is a form of minor agreement that something important is being said and should be heard out. It may also make the attacker more conscious of the message's volume, stress, and content. In addition it avoids confrontations in which we say too much, only to regret it later.

Silence, however, typically leads to anxiety and may be difficult to maintain. By knowing what we will say when the attacker runs out of steam, we should be able to continue listening. Most attackers will be startled by our asking for more and they will back off.

Have you noticed that many of these disarming techniques come in the form of a question? The reason? It's simple. Who controls a conversation? The talker or the listener? When we're attacked, questions help us regain control and get the information we need to solve the problem that triggered the attack.

"We Seem to Have a Problem, Let's Work on It Together."

Even silence and a request for more information may not work, of course. Some attackers may forge onward with "And what do you have to say for yourself?" or make still more personal criticisms. In response to parentlike communications, we may wish to shift the focus from a personal assault to a search for solutions. Here again the key is to agree, but only with part of the message.

We can always agree that the problem is a difficult one and suggest, "We seem to have a problem, let's work on it together." This shows we want to resolve the difficulty and asks for the other person's cooperation in finding solutions.

When all else fails, it may be best to retreat from the heat in the hopes of reconnecting when things cool down.

Setting Others Free

The aikido described above is very useful when the anger a stressed-out person feels is expressed as a verbal fight. At times, however, the anger is expressed as a passive-aggressive form of flight. Some people withdraw, but keep looking back over their shoulders hoping you're upset by their departure. Perhaps they want to defy the maxim that no one is indispensable.

Once again it is important to avoid taking the vanishing act personally. At first we may feel rejected when someone walks away. It may remind some of us of the way our parents punished us by seeming to withdraw their love when we were particularly naughty.

"It Seems Like You Need Some Space Right Now ... and That's Okay."

Even if the person is trying to avoid us, bait us, or punish us, our best response is to recognize that she needs her space and to give her some room as a gift. In this way we are simply not enabling her to control us with her withdrawal. We refuse to let the invisible domino clobber us.

Nothing is worse for some people than retreating and finding that no one notices. Often they will come back just to see what is going on.

We recommend that the stressed-out person always be given "the right of way." If someone is withdrawing, it may help to say calmly, "I've noticed that you haven't been too communicative lately. It seems like you might need some space right now. If that's true, I just want you to know that's okay with me." In this way we acknowledge his apparent need and give him permission to do what he is already doing.

If the stressed-out person is playing a game of hide-and-seek, however, this will take all the fun out of it. We have essentially disarmed her by once again agreeing with her. We might follow up with "Seems like you need some space. I respect that, but I want you to know that the door is open."

If his withdrawal is intended as an underhanded, invisible blow, the game is up and the person will be forced to find a more effective, hopefully more direct way of communicating. We've told him to have a good trip and that we'll be there when he gets back. Hopefully he'll take our open-door, face-saving offer and come back sooner rather than later. If the withdrawal is simply a need for privacy, we've respected that need. Neither of us can lose, as long as power and control were not the goals.

"Humor Me, Is There Anything Else Going On?"

Let's say we need something from a stressed-out person who has retreated angrily or withdrawn coldly. We may do best simply to set him or her free and accept the consequences as an investment in improving the relationship. Most of the time the stressed-out people will also lose something, and this will decrease the likelihood of similar passive-aggressive behavior in the future.

If we are sure there is something festering, we might try asking, "Humor me, is there anything else going on?" We've essentially sidestepped some of the hostility and communicated that we don't take life so seriously as to be upset by their actions. Once again we've set them free; this time we've set them free of terminal seriousness. It can be surprisingly disarming. Try it.

Agree-or-Set-Free

Whenever a stressed-out person expresses anger through fight-flight-or-freeze, it is important to remember the basics of verbal aikido. It may help to memorize the rhyme "agree-or-set-free." In addition, by practicing this in our mind's eye, we can develop the agility to disarm a verbal attacker or to set free an escape artist.

4

The Power
of Social Support

"Loneliness is the ultimate poverty."
—ABIGAIL VAN BUREN ("DEAR ABBY")

Mary was finishing up the dinner dishes when Sara, her neighbor, called. Sara had just driven back from the hospital where her son, Bobby, had been fighting pneumonia for two weeks.

Not long ago Bobby was winning soccer games for the local high school. Mary had heard that Bobby might be HIV positive. She suspected that his pneumonia was the beginning of AIDS.

Mary wanted to say something that would ease Sara's burden, but she wasn't supposed to know Bobby's real illness. She couldn't think of anything meaningful to say.

Mary felt awkward and cut off from Sara. She was afraid that she sounded cold and impersonal on the phone. Worst of all, she was sure that Sara must be feeling lost and alone.

No One Should Have to Fly Solo

Have you ever heard honking in the sky and looked up to see dozens of geese flying gracefully in a V-shaped formation? Ever wondered why?

Geese can fly hundreds of miles farther in formation than alone. In this way some flocks can fly over a thousand miles without resting. The formation adds over 70 percent more flying range because the flapping wings of each bird creates an uplifting air current for the bird that follows.

Geese rotate their positions when tired. If a bird becomes sick or injured, a pair of helpers fall out of the formation to provide help and protection. No goose has to face the drag and resistance of trying to make it alone.

As humans we are also programmed as social beings. Even ancient nomads moved in groups, but today many of us move alone, in couples, or just with our children. As a result we have fewer established relationships and fewer extended family contacts than our parents enjoyed.

Like Sara we bear our sorrows in isolation because we are afraid to trust our neighbors. Like Mary we are afraid to intrude. We also know fewer people with whom to share our joys. All of this seriously affects our health and our sense of well-being.

Loneliness Is a Health Hazard

When we have no one to turn to and feel alone, we have lost what scientists call social support. The effect on health is dramatic.

An article in *Science* summarized a half-dozen population studies looking at the long-term effects of social support on the lives of more than forty thousand people both here and abroad. The studies controlled for other known risk factors including age, initial health status, and personality variables. The conclusion? Lack of social support was a major risk factor for early death. It was even more powerful than cigarette smoking.

Research suggests that social support can reduce the amount of medication required to manage pain, speed recovery from illness, and shorten the length of hospital stays. It appears that having social support during pregnancy and labor can protect against complications, move the process along faster, and decrease the chances of a woman's needing surgery to give birth.

Other studies demonstrate that broken social ties are associated with many specific diseases, from arthritis to depression, tuberculosis to heart disease. For example six months after a heart attack, patients living alone were nearly twice as likely as those with companions to have another attack—or die of one. These results were quite striking, and even when the researchers double-checked, none of the known risk factors for second heart attacks, including medications, age, and sex, could account for the results.

We Don't Have to Be Sick to Benefit from Social Support

Ohio State University medical students volunteered their blood a month before and on the day of examinations to see the effects of stress on the body's disease-fighting immune system. The students also took the UCLA Loneliness Scale, a paper-and-pencil test that measures feelings of social isolation. The immune functions of all the students were suppressed under stress, but those scoring high on loneliness had the most dramatic effects.

Studies with animals support these findings and offer explanatory clues. In one study cancer cells injected into mice caged alone multiplied faster than the same cells injected into mice caged together.

In another experiment scientists looked at the effects of stress on monkeys when they are alone, in pairs, and in a group. When monkeys are exposed to electric shock, their adrenal glands release cortisol. In monkeys and in people cortisol conserves energy in a crisis, but in the process it decreases the effectiveness of the immune system to fight invaders and to regulate itself.

By presenting the electric shock with a flashing light, the scientists conditioned the monkeys to react stressfully just to the light. This made the experiment a little more humane and controlled for other variables. Now the payoff.

When a monkey alone in a cage was stressed, there was a dramatic rise in cortisol. Adding a second monkey cut this rise in cortisol by almost half. With five fellow sufferers there was no rise at all.

Family Ties to Wellness

In the past the family provided a natural source for social support. Unfortunately families are falling apart. As the number of single-parent homes increases, the losses mount. A survey of seventeen thousand children showed that those living apart from a biological parent are sick 20 to 40 percent more of the time and are 20 to 30 percent more likely to be injured in an accident. It doesn't stop there. Three of four teen suicides occur in broken families.

Supporting the family has traditionally been a function of the religious community. Today churches and synagogues often become convenient places for meeting new people rather than spiritual places for deepening long-standing relationships. When we need support, few of us can turn to stable groups whose members care about us.

It is clear that we all need each other and that those alone risk their well-being and even their lives. Friends and family may be the best health insurance we can find.

Social Support at Work

Stress undermines our ability to learn, our productivity, and our relationships. Comparing the responses of residents near the damaged Three Mile Island nuclear power plant to those living near undamaged power plants, psychologists documented not only fewer symptoms of illness and depression among those with high social support but better performance on a number of tasks requiring concentration and attention.

Most of us need the commitment and cooperation of others to concentrate and achieve success on the job. We may also find co-workers to be a major source of social support. As James A. Autry, a former magazine publishing executive, reveals in *Love and Profit*, the workplace may be our new neighborhood. And friends and co-workers may be the new extended family.

Community has been defined as a group of people living in the same place and under the same body of law. Now many of us consider our work environments to be our community. It is at work that we create stable relationships, interact daily with the same people, and participate in shared activities. At work we are connected in meaningful ways.

Support Groups

Another growing source of social support for many is found in self-help groups. In 1990, fifteen million Americans attended one or more of some half-million weekly support-group meetings. By far the largest support group is Alcoholics Anonymous. AA has become a well-accepted and standard treatment for alcoholism.

A ten-year Stanford study of terminally ill cancer patients found that those who received medical treatment and participated in weekly support groups lived nearly twice as long as those receiving medical treatment alone. This should not be surprising. Independent studies have shown reduced immune activity in breast-cancer patients with few friends.

The needs for social support are so great for some people that there are even reports of a group forming for people who go to support groups too much. As cardiologist Dean Ornish, M.D., points out, it is unfortunate that in our culture people have to have an illness or an alcohol problem to find a community of people for open communication and support.

Both Mary and Sara would benefit if Mary would take the risk of gently opening the communications between them. By learning the H.E.L.P. technique, Mary will develop the confidence to take this risk and support her neighbor.

Being Specific About Social Support

Does social support mean just being around a lot of people? You may recall that in an earlier chapter we showed how crowding creates stress! Does having an extended family guarantee social support? One of our workshop participants answered, "No way." She continued, "When I'm stressed-out, the last person I want around is my mother. First she'll get upset that I'm upset. Then she'll want to know why I did what I did. By the time I finish talking with her, I feel totally inadequate and furious with myself for letting her get to me.

"Even if I don't tell her what's happening, I feel bad," she added, "because I wish I could—but she really doesn't listen and she just can't understand. So I need to stay away."

Social support means a way of providing positive information that helps people reassess or redefine their view of themselves, their situation, or the *quality* of their relationships. Social support is a way of bringing out the good stuff and helping people feel competent and connected.

Quality, Not Quantity

Yes, social support is more than just having people around us. We need people who help us feel cared for and cared about. And it's not just the getting but the giving that is important to health and healing.

When we are providing social support for others, we feel good. When we are able to find something to say that lets the other person know that we understand and care, we connect in a meaningful way. Sometimes there are things that we can do. Sometimes we just have to listen. Sometimes we only have to be there.

Knowing that we are important to the other person and that we are being supportive enhances our self-esteem and does good things for our own health.

Helping Is Healthy

In one of the many population studies that confirmed the powerful link between a lack of social support and early death, researchers divided over 1,300 men of Tecumseh, Michigan, into those who gave volunteer service and those who did not. The finding ten years later? Those who were not volunteering died at two and a half times the rate of those who were volunteering.

To study the effects of helping and caring on the immune system, psychologist David McClelland conducted a fascinating experiment at Harvard using a fifty-minute film on Nobel Laureate Mother Teresa doing good works among the sick and the dying in Calcutta. The movie showed her expressing a kind of selfless love for abandoned babies and the poor.

Before and after showing the film, McClelland took a small saliva sample from 132 Harvard students and analyzed changes in immunoglobulin A (S-IgA), an antibody that defends against the cold virus. Surprisingly, whether the students admired Mother Teresa's work, distrusted her religiosity, or dismissed her efforts as futile, their saliva still contained a significant increase in immunoglobulin A. The conclusion: Even observing or learning about someone else's helping behavior affects our immune system and may be protective for our health.

Later research at Harvard studied the effects on health of a specific characteristic that Mother Teresa's courageous work embodies, a trait called affiliative trust. People with affiliative trust have a desire to care about and connect with other people. In addition they have nothing specific that they need to achieve. Compared to students scoring low on affiliative trust, students scoring high on the trait had stronger helper-to-suppressor T-cell ratios, another measure of a healthy immune system. Perhaps more important, ten years after assessment those high in affiliative trust reported suffering significantly fewer major illnesses.

The Helper's High

In *The Healing Power of Doing Good* Allan Luks reported the results of his survey of 3,296 volunteers from more than twenty organizations across the country. Luks found that the more frequent the volunteering, the greater the health benefits. "There was a ten times greater chance that volunteers who said they were healthier than others would be weekly [helpers] rather than once-a-year helpers."

Of the volunteers, 95 percent reported that helping another person gives them an immediate physical response involving sudden warmth, increased energy, and/or euphoria. Luks calls this the helper's high. This rush is then followed by increased feelings of self-worth, calm, and relaxation. There is even some intriguing laboratory research with dogs relating this helper's rush to the better-known runner's high. The same morphinelike brain opioids, including the endorphins, may be involved.

All of these studies are complex and preliminary, but the

trend is clear: Helping is healthy and it makes us feel good. In the next chapter we will try to understand why more people don't take advantage of these healthy opportunities to bond and help.

5

Social Support
Sounds Great, But . . .

"Life is short and we have not too much time for gladdening the hearts of those who are traveling the dark way with us. Oh, be swift to love! Make haste to be kind."

—HENRI AMIEL

Imagine that you are visiting Princeton University, a campus of wide green lawns and magnificent stone structures. You see a young student of religion leaving one building and rushing through an alley on his way to another. A shabbily dressed man is sitting slumped in a doorway, head down, eyes closed, and not moving. As the seminarian approaches, the man, in obvious distress, coughs twice and groans. The student hesitates but continues on and takes a left turn out of the alley.

Fifteen minutes later another seminary student passes through the alley and proceeds to step over the victim as he dashes between the buildings. Would you believe that the second seminarian was on his way to give a talk about the parable of the Good Samaritan?

In the parable, you may recall, Jesus tells how a priest and a religious man, a Levite, see a man who was robbed, lying half dead on the side of the road. Each in turn passes the victim by, but a religious outcast, a Samaritan, stops and helps him. Jesus instructs his followers to "Go and do likewise." What does this have to do with the seminary students?

Princeton professors John M. Darley, a psychologist, and C. Daniel Batson, a theologian, brought the biblical tale back to life in the early 1970s. They wanted to find out what sort of characteristics and situations motivate people to engage in helping behavior. So they added a twist. The professors randomly chose twenty seminary students to give a talk about the Good Samaritan and another twenty to give a talk about jobs for graduates. Furthermore a third of the students were told that they were "late" for the talk, a third that they needed to "go right over," and a third that it'd "be a few minutes" before things would be ready for the talk.

The results were surprising. Of the forty seminarians, only sixteen offered some form of help to the distressed man they passed in the alley. The topic of the talk they were about to give did not make a significant difference, but their time urgency was an important variable. In the low-hurry condition 63 percent helped; in the medium-hurry, 45 percent; and in the high-hurry, only 10 percent.

Of course, there are many ways to interpret these results. After all, the seminarians were already helping the professors, and perhaps there was a conflict between loyalties rather than callousness, which could explain some of their actions. In fact later statistical reanalysis showed that preparing to give a talk about the parable did increase the odds in favor of helping by more than 50 percent. However, the most compelling predictor of helping clearly involved time—whether or not the student was in a hurry. This brings us to the first reason why we often fail to support stressed-out people in our lives: We are stressed-out ourselves, because of a variety of urgent demands. So we are less open to seeing or hearing others' needs and have fewer resources for helping.

As the researchers wrote, "One can imagine the priest and Levite, prominent public figures, hurrying along with little

black books full of meetings and appointments, glancing fur-
tively at their sundials."

Studying Bystanders

We've all read about incidents where victims desperately
needed help but people stood on the sidelines or drove on.
Sadly the list seems to grow longer every day: Someone robs
a taxicab driver, assaults an old woman, or discriminates
against a person of color, and no one cares. Have Americans
become depersonalized, unconcerned, and uncaring?

Studies of people who hear someone having an epileptic sei-
zure in a nearby room and people who find themselves in an
area beginning to fill with smoke show that the size of the
group and the responses of others to the emergency, rather
than altruistic personality traits, seem to determine their behavior. The problem must be noticed, accurately interpreted,
and determined to involve personal responsibility before most
people will intervene.

It's not that people have become cold and indifferent.
Sometimes they're afraid. Often they agonize about the decision but fail to act.

The lesson for social support should be clear. Don't assume
others are helping a stressed-out person. Reach out with some
help and find out if the other person needs support.

"I Don't Always Have Time to Listen"

Annette is a busy accountant with two young children. She
has made several unsuccessful calls to convince one of her clients to review some tax returns. Annette's client, Laurie, is a
marketing executive who has managed to break through the
glass ceiling at a Fortune 500 company. Annette recently
learned from a friend that Laurie had just separated from her
husband of eight years. Annette feels bad about the situation
but has been careful not to ask any questions.

As her accountant, Annette wants to respect Laurie's privacy. She considers personal situations to be taboo subjects. More important, having helped a sister through a messy divorce, Annette is afraid that if she asks how things are going, she would be inundated by a flood of tears and detailed information. She remembers spending countless hours and many entire evenings with her sister during the acute stage of her confusion and grief.

Annette is right; people can become a burden if we don't know how to limit the time we spend with them and still help them to feel competent and connected.

Less Is More

It may surprise you to learn, as it did Annette, that for the most part, the more time you spend, the less effectively you will communicate. In some ways, encouraging people to go on and on about their situation can increase their sense of helplessness, victimization, and resentment. Have you ever noticed that when you get upset, the more you describe the details of the insults and injuries you've suffered, the angrier you get? Or perhaps you've noticed that the more you moan, the more depressed you get? Repeating the gruesome details of the story triggers the hurt and anger all over again.

Most people believe more is better, and unfortunately when it doesn't work as expected, they do even more of it.

Healthy communications increase the other person's sense of personal control and support from you. By bringing the situation sharply into focus and expressing your caring but limiting the discussion, you communicate two things. First, that you believe the other person to be capable of managing the problem. Second, that you manage your time and energy in such a way that if he or she needs more support, you'll have the resources to provide it.

"Maybe It's None of My Business"

Annette may have been concerned mostly about her time, but you may be more concerned about meddling in someone's personal life. It's hard to support people unless we can find out what is troubling them. At the same time we don't want to invade their privacy.

Sally's Dilemma

After four years as Mr. Jackson's administrative secretary, Sally had a good working relationship with her boss. Over the years she had come to know his wife and children from their visits to the office. Sally enjoyed an occasional lunch with Mr. Jackson when he ordered in, and they would usually have a cup of coffee together a couple of times a week.

One Wednesday Mr. Jackson came to work looking upset. His face was pale and he passed the receptionist without his usual cheerful greeting. He walked directly into his office and pulled the door shut with an emphatic snap. He was more demanding of everyone throughout the day, questioning details of reports, grumbling exaggerated criticisms, and issuing orders in areas he usually delegated. Sally was grateful when it was finally time to go home.

By Friday afternoon Sally knew something was very wrong. Mr. Jackson seemed preoccupied and unresponsive, even when the president of the company poked his head in the door to ask how things were going on a major account.

Later, when she brought Mr. Jackson some papers, she hesitated before leaving and asked him, "Are you okay?" He mumbled, "Yes, I guess so," but then inquired if anyone in her family had ever been involved with drugs. Sally shook her head no, and asked, "Why?"

Before she knew it, she had learned about Mr. Jackson's brother, a drug user with AIDS, who'd been arrested earlier in the week for selling cocaine. Sally also learned about his mother's history of mental illness, her untimely visit, and his wife's dislike for his family. Mr. Jackson asked Sally to call him Bob and thanked her for being so supportive.

It was almost six-thirty when Sally left the office. She couldn't stop thinking about Mr. Jackson's problems and told her husband, Sam, all the details so that he would understand why she was upset. Sam serves on the local American Heart Association board with Mr. Jackson's wife and was relieved when she wasn't at the meeting on Saturday. That afternoon, while Sam was playing golf, one of his buddies brought up the arrest. Sam revealed that Sally worked for the man's brother and that it was a real family mess.

During the next week Sally tried to call Mr. Jackson "Bob" and to support him as much as she could. She got behind in her work but decided that the most important thing she could do was to get her boss back on his feet.

Some of their talks lasted hours and were not very productive. Sally didn't know what to say or do. Certainly her secretarial school had never taught her how to handle these situations.

Should she give Bob advice, agree with his solutions, suggest he see a counselor, or call in sick? Mainly she just listened. Bob's family situation was somewhat like her own. Her husband never got along with her father, who had been an alcoholic. Early memories started to flood her waking hours, and she began having some disturbing dreams. She lived for the weekends, when she was able to get away from Bob's problems.

About three weeks later Sally was relieved to hear that Mr. Jackson's brother was out on bail, his mother had safely returned to Wisconsin, and all was well in the Jackson marriage. But now Bob seemed cold and distant. Sally didn't know whether to call him Bob or Mr. Jackson. She felt angry and a little used. After a while the relationship returned to a seminormal state with only a little chill remaining between them, but somehow Sally no longer trusted Mr. Jackson.

What Went Wrong?

Sally's dilemma is a very common one. Mr. Jackson was in the throes of serious family problems and went on tilt. He became more irritable, demanding, needy, and dependent. His distress was within the normal range and not evidence of a personality disorder, but it was felt by his boss and his subordinates, especially by Sally.

Mr. Jackson sought more help and nurturance from a relationship than it was created to provide. Some might think that this could be a wonderful opportunity to enhance their relationship, but Sally found it difficult to handle without becoming overinvolved.

Like most people Sally and Mr. Jackson had developed a pattern of working together. They exchanged pleasantries and provided each other with a sense of community. The level of intimacy was superficial, but comfortable and functional. Mr. Jackson's family problems changed the character of their interactions, carrying all sorts of confidences that had no place in a business relationship or in Sally's or her husband's lives. Sally didn't know what to do with Mr. Jackson's emotional confessions and family crisis.

Once Mr. Jackson stepped over the normal boundaries, Sally became upset. Her territory and time had been invaded, and the situation put her painfully in touch with some of her own family issues.

Sally's husband played "ain't it awful" with both Sally and his golfing friends. Gossiping initially made him feel important, but ultimately he and his buddies all felt a little uncomfortable knowing that their own privacy could be exposed under similar circumstances.

When the acute phase of the problem was over, Sally experienced a backlash as Mr. Jackson pushed their relationship too far in the opposite direction to compensate for a work relationship that he feared had become too intimate.

Avoiding Intimacy Traps by Providing H.E.L.P.

The problems we just described are very common. This may explain why so many people are hesitant to support the stressed-out people in their lives.

Is it possible to communicate support and not end up in emotional quicksand? Yes, but we need to clarify where we want to go, overcome our fears, and use the best ways of getting there.

There are effective ways of offering support without invading a person's privacy. First, using the H.E.L.P. technique explained in the next chapter, our focus will be on what people are experiencing rather than the details of their private lives. Second, even under stress, people will usually adjust the depth of personal information they share to the level of our relationship with them. Finally, we will look at easy ways of redirecting the person should the content become too heavy.

"No One Ever Listens to My Advice Anyway"

If you find that people don't listen to your advice, you are in very good company. Most people don't take other people's advice. In fact our advice about giving advice is simple: Don't give it.

Some people think they are generous because they give away free advice. Unfortunately by giving advice we usually undermine the self-confidence of the recipients. Alternatively, by allowing others to find their own way we can truly support, respect, and empower them.

At a recent workshop Janice, a lively, dark-eyed mother of two teenagers, whose husband recently separated from her, confirmed this. She volunteered, "I'm crazy about my friend Claire. I can relax when I'm with her. I know she's not going to tell me what to do or give me any advice."

"*What If I'm Stressed Out Myself?*"

As we saw earlier in the experiments on helping behavior, being stressed-out ourselves is one of the more common reasons for our insensitivity to other people's problems. We need to recognize that like everyone else, when we don't feel in control or competent, we go on tilt. Each of us has to take responsibility for monitoring and managing our personal stress.

We are never required to respond to a stressed-out person. This is particularly important to remember whenever trying to respond is likely to put us on tilt or over the edge. If we don't take care of ourselves first, we can't take care of others. The H.E.L.P. technique introduced in the next chapter offers us a wonderful way of changing feelings of helplessness, whether our own or others', into feelings of control.

"*Okay, but How Much Time* Will *Giving H.E.L.P. Take?*"

How does five minutes sound? Connecting with people using our H.E.L.P. system should take as few as five minutes. After this investment of time the other person will be calmer and far more open to hearing other things that you may need to tell him. You won't have to repeat yourself as often.

So, once mastered, the H.E.L.P. system is not going to cost you time. On the contrary, it will save you time.

PART II

The Basics:
It H.E.L.P.S.
to
Communicate
Effectively

6

How to H.E.L.P.
and Support
Stressed-Out People

"Most of the time we don't communicate, we just take turns talking."

—Author unknown

Take number two: Bill hadn't seen Joe around the office for a few weeks, so when he saw him in the cafeteria, he took his coffee and headed in his direction. Joe looked terrible. There were dark circles under his eyes and his clothes were wrinkled.

As Bill came closer, Joe motioned for him to sit down. Bill needed to get back to some important paperwork, but there was no way to escape Joe's obvious invitation and need.

"Good to see you, Joe. What's happening in your life?" Bill asked. Joe took a deep breath before responding.

"You won't believe this, Bill, but Kathy's left me. After twenty-one years, after raising the kids and everything we've been through together, she just up and left me." Whatever color there was in Joe's face before Bill sat down was now gone.

Bill contained his curiosity. He knew that learning the gruesome details might be embarrassing later. Besides, given his schedule and Joe's appearance, he did not want to hear the long version of the story. Actually Bill and Joe had never been close, just co-workers who played an occasional game of racquetball, so Bill also didn't want Joe to tell him things that he might later regret sharing with him.

After pausing briefly Bill asked, "Wow, how'd it make you feel?"

Joe grit his teeth and clenched his fist before replying, "I was so angry, I wanted to kill her."

Bill was feeling uncomfortable. He wondered if he'd gotten in too deep after all. Having listened intensely, though, he was able to reflect back, "Looks like . . . what you're telling me . . . is that you were totally unprepared for Kathy's leaving you and now you're feeling angry and resentful."

Joe nodded his head very slowly. Then, looking directly at Bill, Joe said, "You got it right there, pal."

Bill thought for a moment before asking, "Joe, do you have any plans now?"

Shaking his head again, Joe said, "I don't know. It's just crazy. It's a mess. And I really don't know what to do."

"I can understand that, Joe, it must be really hard for you." Bill was being as supportive as he knew how. He was letting Joe know that he saw him reacting appropriately to a very bad situation.

"Yeah, but I'm getting some help from the employee assistance program and I'm hanging in there," said Joe. Bill leaned over and put his hand on Joe's shoulder. "Sounds like you're doing the best you can with some pretty tough stuff. Let's plan to get together soon."

"Hey," said Joe, brightening up a bit, "you know, we haven't played racquetball for a while. It would do me good to run around a court and beat up on a ball."

"Sounds great," said Bill, getting up and feeling both a little relieved and very pleased that he'd been able to support a friend. "How about Saturday morning?" Joe's nod and smile said it all as they went back to their offices.

Bill was pleased. He had just gotten the opportunity to apply the H.E.L.P. and Support technique that he learned in one of our workshops.

What Bill Was Able to Avoid

Not only was the encounter brief and supportive, it left Joe with his dignity and his privacy. Bill was able to help without learning things that Joe might later regret telling him.

When any important relationship breaks up, but especially when a marriage shatters, part of the emotional fallout consists of angry and hurt feelings. There are also needs to justify or find reasons why the relationship could not survive. These details are best left to the parties involved. We can express our confidence—meaning that we believe the other person is competent and will in time handle the problem. We can also connect with the person—meaning that we are choosing to spend time, share a meal, or comfort him. To support people in these ways, however, we do not have to become a recipient of private details that they may later regret sharing. When people are on tilt, they often regress into very early, dependent positions, and if someone opens the floodgates, they will spill everything.

In this case Bill might have learned about Joe and Kathy's long-standing sexual dysfunction and his drinking problems. Fortunately Bill maintained the boundaries and yet communicated genuine caring and support.

Doing What H.E.L.P.S.

The shortest and surest path we know to connecting supportively with someone in crisis is to use the following series of questions and comments. In addition this path can be taken for self-support and is the foundation for a wider and more advanced approach to communicating. We will talk more about this later.

Since strong emotions are contagious and may interfere with memory, we also developed a way to help rapidly recall each step in the system. Note that each question or comment contains one or two key words that begin with a letter in the acronym H.E.L.P.S. When we need to use what H.E.L.P.S., the letters enable us to remember and use it confidently and effectively.

Steps on the Path to H.E.L.P. and Support

HAPPENING:	"What's Happening in your life?"
EMOTION:	"How are you feeling (emotionally) about that?" / "What Effect is this having on you?"
LISTENING:	"It Looks like you are feeling ____ about ____."
PLAN/PERMISSION:	"What's your Plan?"/"That must must be very painful for you."

Adding <u>Support</u> and Doing What HELPS

HAPPENING

EMOTION

LISTENING

PLAN/PERMISSION

SUPPORT: "Sounds like you're doing the best you can with a difficult **Situation**."

H Is for <u>H</u>appening

Do you know the best way to find out what's happening with people? The answer is surprisingly simple but often overlooked—ask them! It is remarkable how often we can spend hours with friends and have no idea what they are really going through. We may have spent time with them, but have no idea of the events unfolding in their lives.

For this reason we start by throwing a net wide enough to catch anything important. To review, Bill opened with "Good to see you, Joe. What's happening in your life?"

E Is for the <u>E</u>motion or the <u>E</u>ffect

When we want to support stressed-out people, the situation that threw them into crisis is surprisingly unimportant. It really doesn't matter what has happened. What's happened is history. How it makes them feel is far more important.

Recognizing this encourages us to move quickly to feelings and reactions. We focus on connecting with the person, not on the often uncontrollable situation. Avoiding excessive, time-consuming, and often private details is an added benefit.

After all, it's the emotional response that makes a crisis a crisis. A person may feel overwhelmed, powerless, depressed, or totally out of control . . . in other words, on tilt. When we ask about a person's feelings, we communicate genuine inter-est. Labeling the emotion is also the first step in regaining control.

The alternative, "What Effect is this having on you?" allows us to indicate our concern about the person's feelings while maintaining a more formal distance. Many people we've worked with are initially uncomfortable asking, "How are you feeling about that?" To some it seems to open the door to an avalanche of feelings. To others it sounds too much like what a therapist might say, so they prefer the alternative "What ef-fect is this having on you?"

The exact words are not critical. The important point is to express our interest and direct our attention to the person's re-action to the situation.

Joe had told Bill that Kathy had left. So, after pausing only briefly, Bill asked, "Wow, how'd it make you feel?"

L Is for Listening

One of the most powerful ways of letting people know that we value them and take them seriously is to really listen. Lis-tening and hearing, however, are not the same. In order to demonstrate that we have really listened, it is important to re-flect back both the feeling and the content that we've just heard. This is called active listening. In "It Looks like you are feeling ____ about ____," the first blank represents the emo-tion, the second represents what's happening. In active listening the emphasis is on the other person. That's the *you* in the sentence above.

This approach is the foundation of an entire school of psychotherapy, called client-centered or Rogerian therapy. When therapists listen with nonjudgmental acceptance and reflect back both content and emotions with accuracy, clients feel genuinely understood. This makes them feel both competent and connected. They feel competent because they know they are communicating clearly. They feel connected because they know the other person continues to accept them after having truly heard their story. This support frees them up to consider other possibilities, make changes in their perceptions, and take some personal risks. In the process measurable growth takes place. In order to apply this listening technique, we have to give people our full attention.

Please note that there are blanks in which to insert what the person has said earlier in response to the *H* and the *E* in H.E.L.P. We fill in these blanks carefully because it is so important for us to hear and reflect accurately the feelings evoked by the crisis.

Having listened intensely, Bill was able to reflect back, "Looks like . . . what you're telling me . . . is that you were totally unprepared for Kathy's leaving you and now you're feeling angry and resentful." Notice that this is one of Bill's more awkward responses, but it works just fine. He got a little stuck because the *L* in H.E.L.P. triggered "Looks like." The words *Looks like* helped him to remember to make a reflection, but there really wasn't any doubt about the event or Joe's reaction.

P Is for Plans, Problem Solving, and Possibilities

Asking people about their Plan invites them to explore their options with us. On the other hand, it also gives them the chance simply to tell us that they have a plan and to communicate that they don't need us to serve as a sounding board at this time. In either case the question continues to express our interest in their personal welfare. It also gives us a chance to assess their decision-making capacities.

P can also stand for _Permission. When people are so overwhelmed that they are unable to make any plans at the moment, it usually makes them feel incompetent and they expect disapproval. When instead they get our acceptance, they feel much better. So one of our goals is to acknowledge and respect people's temporary inabilities. It's bad enough to be depressed without being put down for being depressed.

On a few occasions we may learn that a friend or co-worker is planning to do something totally self-defeating or even self-destructive. This is a good thing for us to find out.

At times we may decide to help the person in a more direct way. We will review the risks and pitfalls of giving advice or fixing things for other people. Later we will also talk about some of the ways to handle potentially self-destructive behaviors.

Bill wondered how seriously he should take Joe's threat that he wanted to kill Kathy. He asked, "Joe, do you have any plans now?"

S Is for _Support

After we have H.E.L.P.ed someone, it is very supportive to acknowledge her plan and her efforts in an affirming way. A wonderful way to do that is to add the S: "_Sounds like you're doing the best you can with a difficult _Situation."

This very simple statement communicates that you have a sense of what is happening to the other person, that you can understand how it might be a difficult situation, and that you think the person is handling it as well as can be expected.

What if we think the person should revise her plan? As long as the plan is not self-destructive, it is probably best not to offer our opinion unless she asks us for it. In addition, looking closely at the S statement above, we are not suggesting that we lie and say that we think it's the best thing to do. The people to whom we supportively say the S statement *are* doing the very best they can, or they would do something better.

Affirming their decision in this way allows them to feel competent and reconnected to their inner resources. With this support they are much more likely to change a faulty plan than if we undermine their confidence by criticizing them or telling them what we think they should do.

When we actively listen to people without passing judgment, we communicate a great deal. Our behavior says that we respect them and care about them.

When we empathize—that is, when we share our accurate understanding of their reactions to their situations—that's powerful stuff! We connect.

Bill expressed empathy twice in the earlier example. When Joe said, "I don't know. It's just crazy. It's a mess. And I really don't know what to do," Bill responded with "I can understand that, Joe, it must be really hard for you." In addition, after Joe told him he was getting help from the employee assistance program, Bill supported that by saying, "Sounds like you're doing the best you can with some pretty tough stuff."

Empathy does not make us responsible for fixing their problems. This would overwhelm us and undermine their self-esteem. Empathy also doesn't mean that we need to reveal our struggles with similar experiences. This would discount their uniqueness and divert attention from them.

Empathy acknowledges our connection with stressed-out people and affirms both their suffering and their strength. Empathy helps people regain their balance when they are on tilt. Empathy heals.

Rehearsing New Responses

Just as we can mentally rehearse the disarming techniques of verbal aikido, we can do the same with each step of H.E.L.P. First we can replay a situation in which we knew someone was stressed-out but we didn't know what to say. Or we can envision someone we know facing a new and difficult crisis. Let's imagine the situation using at least sight and sound. If we can, let's add touch, smell, or taste to increase our involvement.

Next let's see the stressed-out person and allow ourselves to experience our initial anxiety. Perhaps "What am I going to do?" runs through our minds. Then let's feel ourselves slowing our breathing and hear ourselves thinking, *What was that key word, oh, yes, H.E.L.P. . . . H was for Happening. . . . I'll ask, "What's happening in your life?"* We can create and then imagine listening carefully to the person's response.

By jogging our memory we can think about the next letter in H.E.L.P. *E* for Emotion, we remember, or we drop the bottom, horizontal line off the *E* and get *F* for Feeling. Then we ask how the person is feeling. If asking this is uncomfortable for us, we can try asking it again several times in our minds. Let's remind ourselves that anything worth doing is worth doing awkwardly the first time. On the other hand, if we have imagined a very formal situation or we are really uncomfortable and ready to bail out of this process entirely, we can try, "What Effect is this having on you?" or "How has this been for you?"

Next we'll imagine thinking *L* for Listening and Looks Like. Let's see the phrase with its empty underlines and fill in the blanks with the person's feeling and the situation.

Now we can go on to the *P* in H.E.L.P.S. First we have to decide if the person is capable of having a Plan to ask about or if it would be better to give Permission by reflecting the person's Pain. Then we can continue this process through to S and Support the person in the Situation. We can also replay this situation and imagine how H.E.L.P.S. would fit different responses from the stressed-out person.

It's Not What We Say, It's How We Say It

By rehearsing H.E.L.P.S. we hope to have made it clear how many different ways we can say the same words. We can vary the tone in our voice, the emphasis we give to different words, or the position of our body as we speak. These nonverbal differences are commonly known as our body language.

Body language often helps us become aware when others are stressed-out. In addition, as we will see in the next chapter, how we say things can be far more important than the words we use.

7

Body Language: Theirs and Ours

"Seeing is believing."
—Anonymous

How do we know people are stressed-out? If they are talking, we can listen to what they say, but studies suggest that less than 35 percent of what people communicate is carried by their words. Body language tells most of the story.

What is body language? It involves everything from eye movement to facial expression, voice tone to body posture. It discloses critical information about emotions and relationships. Even barely perceptible behaviors can carry meaning. Research shows that in as little as a 1/24th of a second, we can recognize the feeling in a person's face.

In the late 1800s Charles Darwin found that facial expressions had universal meaning. Wherever he traveled, gladness pulled the ends of the mouth upward, and the faces of anger, disgust, fear, surprise, and happiness looked nearly the same, regardless of culture or country.

What's in a Smile?

Want to know how a person is feeling? Look at his or her face. If a person's words contradict their facial expression, listen to what their face is telling you. It is difficult to fake a feeling. A genuine feeling flows quickly across the face. People who try to hide pain with a smile usually smile at the wrong time or hold the expression for too long.

How can we tell the differences between real and fake smiles? A real one is a quick one. It rises up into the eyes and invades the top of the face. A false smile looks plastered on the bottom of the face and is usually not as wide as a true smile.

When things don't seem to add up, we know something's wrong. Most of us observe these nonverbal discrepancies automatically. Some call this intuition, but it's nothing magical.

Research shows that women are more accurate than men at decoding body language, but motivation and practice can overcome these differences. When you have a funny feeling about someone, pay attention to it. See if you can figure out what's bothering you and why. Look for mismatches between the person's verbal and nonverbal behavior.

Mix and Match

Clothing may also provide nonverbal clues, but they are sometimes deceptive. People may wear bright clothing both to pick themselves up when they are down and to give others a different impression of how they feel. Other nonverbal language may be more revealing, so it's best to gather enough pieces of the puzzle to see the full picture.

We've talked a little about ways stressed-out people may cover pain with a forced smile or a special outfit, but what about anger? Are there subtle clues you can use to spot anger before it erupts?

Territoriality

We wrote earlier about the effects of crowding on animal behavior and how it often led to violence. Most of us need our space too. It's an invisible, protective boundary, a cushion or "bubble" for us. When someone insults or angers us, our bubbles expand in size. Studies of violent criminals show that their bubbles are larger than nonviolent criminals and tend to bulge back as if to protect them from rear attacks.

The saying "Proximity reflects intimacy" applies here. If someone is "keeping their distance," they may fear us, but they may also be angry with us. We need to be prepared to use verbal aikido.

Of course we can overinterpret and misinterpret the silent language of space. Studies show that sex, age, and ethnic origin influence our needs for space. There are "contact cultures," for instance, Latins and Arabs, who tend to talk and interact closely, touching frequently. There are also "noncontact cultures," for instance Americans and Europeans, who need more distance and less touching. Even among Americans, whites generally prefer more conversational space than blacks. Keep an open mind, but if someone backs away from you, don't pursue them, set them free.

Keep Your Body Language Soft

Body language is fun and informative to observe, but when it comes to coping with stressed-out people, we'd better be watching our own. In addition, as always, we have far more control over our own actions than those of others.

If we are coming under a loud, angry verbal attack and want to disarm the stressed-out person, we need to plan the intensity and tone of our voice carefully. The tendency is to respond with the same or greater volume, speed, and tension. Even if we use the right words, our voices can override their meaning and escalate the conflict.

The best way to make our words and body language match is to hold fast to our goals of expressing calm concern and finding good solutions. It's time to turn down both the volume and the tension. We should also slow the pace. At the same time we need to avoid putting special emphasis on any of the words we use. Instead we can use belly breathing both to relax our vocal cords and to add warmth to all our words.

When someone is angry, it's also important to keep our distance and avoid touch. Angry people need space. Without caring words, touch conveys power and only adds to the struggle for control.

On the other hand, when a person is in pain and we want to offer H.E.L.P., we can use closeness to connect and touch to comfort. Body language is extremely important in communicating empathy, warmth, and caring.

The Eyes Have It

Eye contact intensifies emotions. If someone threatens us, we should avoid cold stares. The total absence of eye contact, however, can signal dishonesty or anxiety.

If we are helping someone, it is best to lean forward. Studies show a twenty-degree lean toward a person communicates liking, attention, and thoughtfulness, regardless of the sex of the one who leans. Counselors who leaned forward in this way increased their clients' perceptions of their attractiveness and warmth.

Other research, however, showed that facial cues can override both a forward lean and good eye contact. In this silent language it seems that the face speaks louder than the body.

Are You Closed or Open?

The face may tell more, but closed arm positions seem to convey coldness, rejection, and inaccessibility, while somewhat open arm positions tend to indicate warmth, attention, and acceptance. In addition to unfolding our arms and legs, we may want to unfurrow our brows and keep our hands away from our chin or mouth. It is said that the mouth signals approval. Covering our mouth while we listen is not only a closed position, it may communicate disapproval of what is said. If we nod, show our smile, and use other nonverbal prompts, such as "Mmm" and "Uh-huh", we will communicate general approval, understanding, and interest.

All of this needs to be taken with many grains of salt. A closed arm position usually signals emotional distance, but it is also a comfortable position.

The Power of Silence

When someone is hurting, our very presence, our "being there," can be enormously supportive. The absence of words gives the stressed-out person much-needed space to think, feel, and speak.

If we rearrange the letters in the word *listen*, we will find one of the keys to all good listening, the word *silent*. We cannot listen unless we are silent. Our body can communicate interest, but if we want someone to become more active and expressive, it is usually best to become more passive and receptive.

Up, Down, and Sideways

Where is the best place to listen? In addition to considering physical distance, we may also need to take height into account when choosing or adjusting our seating arrangement. We look up to impartial judges who sit across courtrooms on elevated benches. Someone who wants our help doesn't need dominance, judgments, or distance. On the other hand, we may wish to invite someone who is attacking us to sit down and talk about the problem. They'll be less intimidating, and we're more likely to see "eye to eye" about the problem.

We may wish to ask an attacker to leave a public setting and go to his or her office, where everyone will feel more comfortable. Try a phrase such as "This seems very important to you, can we discuss it in your office?" Even if territoriality is not an issue, we would do best to consider needs for privacy, sunlight, and ventilation when choosing a room. Developing our sensitivity to these variables can add immensely to everyone's needs for safety and support.

Revisiting the Windows to the Soul

Let's return to eye contact, as we should whenever we want to connect and offer support. Research shows that the more we look at a person during a conversation, the more that person will report feeling liked by us. When people feel liked, they feel competent and connected. They feel support.

So how much time do we maintain eye contact during an average conversation? Studies report that we connect visually about a third of the time. Two women conversing look directly at each other almost twice as long as two men, but in mixed company we all average 31.5 percent.

Are there limits? Of course. Lovers can average three-quarters of their conversational time and feel comfortable, but otherwise it can become oppressive or intimidating.

Mirroring for Rapport

Ever watch the body language of two close friends or a couple while they talk? They move together. When one leans forward, the other leans forward. They mirror each other. When one crosses his or her legs, the other does the same. It's almost a dance. If you listen to the speed and tone of one, you'll hear it like an echo from the other.

Sometimes this harmony is called rapport. We can deliberately increase our connectedness with other people by modifying our body language to match theirs. The closer the match,

the stronger the connection. But beware. If we imitate someone too much, they may feel that we are mocking them. Mir-
roring must be subtle to be effective. Fortunately it seldom
works very long when misused for personal gain rather than to
achieve a caring oneness.

Using Body Language to Say Good-bye

We can also use body language to help us express the
amount of time we have to support people. When we remain
standing, we communicate that the interaction must be limited
to a few minutes. At other times, when we stand up, walk
them to the door, and even to their car, it firmly communicates
that we have done what we can and that we believe in their
competence to survive without us.

Why We Don't Need to Memorize Body Language

How can we remember all these aspects of body language?
Each channel, from voice tone to eye contact, posture to distance, can prove interesting and valuable. Fortunately, unlike
the steps in H.E.L.P., there is a high level of repetition across
nonverbal channels, and all these channels tend to work in
concert. What one channel broadcasts is parallel to what another communicates. Change one and you'll probably change
others. In addition body language is so powerful that a little
goes a long way. Politicians know this all too well.

Huey Long's brother once explained the colorful Louisiana
governor's approach this way: "Don't write anything you can
phone. Don't phone anything you can talk face-to-face. Don't
talk anything you can smile. Don't smile anything you can
wink. And don't wink anything you can nod."

There is still one more good reason you don't have to memorize the whole dictionary of body language. Body language
reflects our genuine feelings. When our intentions are to
H.E.L.P., and we feel comfortable and confident doing so, our

body language communicates these feelings. And when our words and posture send the same messages, people feel our sincerity.

What About Touch?

Physical touch is central to psychological, social, and physical health. It can communicate reassurance, value, and caring at a profound level. It is also a very touchy subject in our culture. We mention it only briefly here because the energy and richness of touch is so great that we devote all of Chapter 23 to it.

In the next section we will illuminate each step of the H.E.L.P. system. As we walk through it, we will point out simple but powerful places in which to use our new fluency in body language. The pace is more leisurely than the last chapter in order to give us time to deepen our understanding of how to apply the system. We will then be prepared to mindfully help others so that we can all enjoy the many rewards of social support.

8

Asking for a Hologram
of What Happened

*"Life is what happens to you while you're busy
making other plans."*

—Author unknown

Ahologram is a three-dimensional picture created by using
a laser. Lasers direct light along a focused beam. Miniature
holograms appear on some credit cards to prevent counterfeit-
ing. Maybe you've seen one of Disney's holographic movies
and ducked when creatures seemed to come right out of the
screen and rush toward you.

Every hologram is complete and unique. Every fragment of
a hologram contains all the information, but in less detail. The
depth of the scene adds realism. Our eyes reconstruct three
dimensions from two images projected from a split laser. One
pattern develops from a reference beam and the other from a
reflected beam. When the two come together, they create an
interference pattern that can be captured and projected to
bring us three-dimensional images.

We may not fully understand how these dramatic pictures
are formed, but, like dominoes, holograms make wonderful

metaphors. Let's see how holograms can help us appreciate the importance of asking stressed-out people what's happening in their lives.

We may recognize that stressed-out people are upset, but we can't know what put them on tilt unless they tell us. Even if we watch an event that is upsetting to someone, we only see the outer, reference beam. We don't see the image created by the inner, reflected beam.

To understand a person's unique situation and grasp its depth, that person must tell us about the inner experience. Only then can we see the whole picture in three dimensions.

Fortunately we don't need a laser. We can use a simple question. But it's a question that can be as direct and powerful as a laser. Asking it can cut through all the fallout from a crisis and open our eyes to the crisis.

The holograms people give us, including both their inner and their outer experiences, will help us see the world through their eyes. Our interest in their perspective dissolves some of the separateness between us. This is the beginning of understanding, empathy, and support.

"What's Happening in Your Life?"

If someone were to ask you right now, "What's going on in your life?" what would you answer? Would you talk about work? School? Family? Relationships? The news? Your weight? Money? The weather? Your automobile? Your vacation? Your health?

Given an interested listener, wouldn't you quickly start talking about a problem or an exciting event? If you were stressed-out, you might answer, "My boss has been making unreasonable demands"; "My son is upset because he didn't make the team"; "My brand-new [fill in the appliance of your choice] died just one day after the warrantee expired"; or any number of other distressing events. Chances are you would feel very good that somebody asked.

Nothing's Happening

People wonder, "What if I ask, but nothing is going on?" There is always something going on. Along with death and taxes, change is guaranteed. We all face not only more change than ever before but a rate of change that is accelerating faster than at any time in history.

Phrases like "There's never a dull moment," "If it's not one thing, it's another," and "You never know what's coming next" capture this experience. If we are not adding or losing family members through birth, death, marriage, or divorce, we are anticipating or recovering from other changes where we live, work, learn, or play. There are always new rules, new roles, and new responsibilities.

Even during an ordinary day small events can carry great significance. One keystroke can send a morning's work into an electronic graveyard. And what about all the other complex and delicate technology in our lives and upon which we have become so dependent? The failure of any number of devices can temporarily affect our entire sense of well-being in the world.

"Please Hear What I'm Not Saying"

When *Parents* magazine commissioned a national opinion poll to find out how people cope with crises, the results were revealing. Only a slight majority of the American public said they would talk to others about them. If they were concerned about losing their job, for example, only 56 percent would turn to their spouses or others for help or support. The fallout from the silence compounds the fallout from the crisis. How often have you heard frustrated people ask, "Well, why didn't you tell me?"

With all the change in people's lives we not only need to ask but we need to ask often. And we need to ask the person directly.

Many people hope to find out what's happening by asking, "How was your day?" All too often the response is an empty "fine" because the question asks for a judgment rather than for information. In contrast "What is happening?" asks the person to choose a topic and to talk about it.

The Importance of "Here and Now"

Suppose we learn through the grapevine what others have heard is going on in someone's life. Even if the information about the event is accurate, it may already have been eclipsed by a new one. If we ask about the "old" event or one we learned about from others, the person could feel both obligated to tell us the end of the story and unsettled by our knowledge of the situation. So if we want to connect with the stressed-out person, it is best to be open to his or her agenda and not to impose our own.

Why do people almost always tell us something that's troubling them instead of something that's bringing them joy? As a species we probably evolved to take the familiar for granted and to quickly assimilate good fortune so that we could focus on potential sources of danger and survive to reproduce. This may be why it is the rare person who focuses on the flowers and not on the weeds of life.

Getting the Gestalt

As we've said, "What's happening in your life?" acts like a wide net that will capture anything of importance. The question is designed to be general rather than specific. Many alternatives have been suggested, such as "What's new in your life?", "What's changed for you since we last spoke?", or "How's your wife?" These are good, general questions, but each has limitations. The stress may not be new, it may not have changed, and a spouse may be divorced or dead.

Many people wonder if they'll get superficial information

about a lot of little happenings. In some ways that doesn't matter, because people nearly always answer the question with something that is bothering them. Why? Gestalt psychology gives us an answer.

The Gestalt school of psychology began by studying perception and gave us the concept of figure and ground. Whatever the person perceives as important at the moment becomes foreground and everything else becomes background. The way we are wired, any immediate or unfinished problem carries a high charge and becomes "figure." Focusing on the figure will help us to solve the problem, gain perspective, or in some way put it to rest. Once we have done so, the problem fades into the background.

Often this process is surprisingly helpful to stressed-out people. By asking the question "What is going on in your life?" we encourage them to separate the wheat from the proverbial chaff. Often we help to make them aware of what is really bothering them.

Gestalt also means "whole." The question helps us get more of the whole picture by asking for their perception.

Most important we are expressing our interest in people and their life experience, their holograms, rather than in their roles. They are not just our friends, relatives, or neighbors; they are not what they do at work; they are people who are reacting to the events and the demands of their lives.

Even if the person answers the question "What's happening in your life?" by saying "Nothing," it can communicate a great deal. Sometimes we can move right on to the "Emotion" in H.E.L.P. and find out how that makes them feel. Another option is to repeat the word "Nothing" with a questioning inflection. Still another is to just wait expectantly. Ninety-nine times out of a hundred the person will start sharing several current happenings. This gives us the opportunity to respond helpfully.

We Can Make the Difference

Why do some people cope well with crises and others fall apart? Over thirty years ago research directed by psychiatrist Gerald Caplan, M.D., at the Harvard University School of Public Health, explored this question. The team studied how a hundred women and their families reacted to a major crisis—the birth of a premature baby who might or might not live.

Trained observers visited each family weekly for two months. Some families weathered the storm successfully, while others were angry, exhausted, and defeated long after the danger had passed. What made the difference?

Was it character? Maturity? No. The key was the kind of help received during the crisis. It was the encouragement by others, by their doctors and friends, to face the danger and experience the stress. Those women who were most upset while their babies hovered between life and death were far better off than the women who tried to deny and avoid their fears. Later studies of critical illness, mourning, and other crises came to similar conclusions.

Thus even in the worst of circumstances, inviting someone to talk about a crisis is kinder than avoiding the topic. In a later chapter, about death and disasters, we will discuss ways of helping people speak the unspeakable fear and bear the unbearable truth without our becoming overwhelmed by anxiety.

Are We Prepared to Hear Bad News?

When we avoid asking or answering the question "What happened?" we may be struggling with larger issues. Something may have happened that challenges our basic beliefs about the safety, predictability, or justness of our world. We may ask, "How could this happen to such a kind and loving person?"

This question of innocent suffering is highly threatening. It reminds us of our own vulnerability. We want to believe the myth that bad things cannot happen to us. In later chapters we will address the feelings we may experience when this belief is challenged. For now, though, let's look briefly at the question of justice.

One of the most comforting, compassionate, and ecumenical of books, *When Bad Things Happen to Good People*, by Rabbi Harold Kushner, addresses this age-old question. Our focus here is less on trying to figure out why things happen and more on finding ways to help us cope.

One approach proposes that life consists of 100 percent neutral events and that the meaning we attribute to circumstances determines our reaction. If we choose to accept this frame of reference, then our task is to accept that things are the way they are and to recognize that if they could be any different, they would be. The choice we make in any situation is an attempt to change the future, but the actual outcome becomes just another event to be accepted. We can also acknowledge that any event presents an opportunity to learn something and to facilitate personal growth.

When we are trying to connect with another person experiencing pain, however, our first task is to find out the circumstances. By treating circumstances as neutral events, we are more open to understanding a person's experiences. This is the beginning of providing H.E.L.P.

In later chapters we will focus on the person's emotional reactions and, still later, the meaning of the event for that person. If we use this process without becoming judgmental or giving advice, we will become more accepting of what happens to ourselves and other people.

Good News, Bad News

Another approach to the injustice of the world is to turn it around and upside down. Surgeon Bernie Siegel tells the following story about psychiatrist Carl Jung. If Jung asked a friend what's happening in his life and the friend answered that he'd gotten a promotion, Carl Jung would say, "Well, maybe if we stick together, we can get you through it." But if the friend answered, "I've been fired," Carl would say, "Wonderful, open a bottle of wine. Something good will come of this."

It sometimes seems impossible to find a silver lining in a cloud, especially while a storm is raging, but it helps to be aware that good things can develop from even the worst of crises. It is not an accident that the Chinese character for *crisis* contains the symbols for both *danger* and *opportunity*.

A recent University of California study supports this view of crises. When volunteers reflected on the most painful experiences of their lives—including serious illness, divorce, or even death of a friend—they reported more positive than negative results. In most cases their trials forced them to reevaluate their goals and redirect their lives in meaningful ways.

Are we suggesting that when people hear bad news, they should take out a bottle of wine or inform people of these research results? No. Not at all. Most stressed-out people will benefit far more from the rest of H.E.L.P. We share these ideas about bad news only in the hope that they will help you to feel more comfortable asking the question "What's happening in your life?" and to feel less anxious when you hear the answers.

Walking a Plank

How can we respond supportively to even the worst disaster? If we've asked the question "What's happening in your life?" we've already begun to give support. Let's clarify what we mean by social support with yet another metaphor.

If a one-foot-wide plank were stretched between two skyscrapers and someone offered you a hundred dollars, would you walk across it? Most people would wisely and understandably decline the opportunity. If the plank were placed on the ground, would your answer change? Of course. You would see and feel the ground under and around you. The narrow width of the plank would not be a threat to your sense of balance because you would see no danger in stepping off. Your confidence would return and you'd probably go away a hundred dollars richer.

The board is like life's journey. When we feel alone and far away from others, we fear that we will fall and that there will be no one there to catch us or pick us up. It is the fear that makes us feel shaky and keeps us from moving onward, not the task. When we face a challenging passage in life alone, it is easy to lose confidence in our abilities and to succumb to our inner doubts.

On the other hand, when there are other people around us, we feel connected. We feel grounded. Their expectations and faith that we make it through the crisis and survive the stress increases our sense of competency. We feel more confident or at least more hopeful that we can make it.

So, like the ground beneath the plank, we can support people by H.E.L.P.ing them to feel connected and competent. Almost everything we recommend is designed to increase these two feelings and thus support others.

How does the question "What's happening in your life?" address these goals of increasing connectedness and competence? When we ask the question, we take the first step toward connecting. Asked in a warm way, it also says, "I want to learn more about you and what you are experiencing." This makes people feel valued and therefore more competent.

Sometimes the person is too busy to answer. We shouldn't assume that our support has not been felt. If we've opened the door, we've done our part.

Anthony, a nurse in one of our workshops, told us of one such incident. It was the beginning of the night shift, when he noticed that a fellow nurse's eyes were bloodshot and half closed. So he said, "You look upset, what's happening?" There was a moment of silence before she stood up and answered,

"Gotta go." At the end of the shift Anthony felt relieved and appreciated when his colleague returned to sort through her anger about a malicious rumor that she thought a third nurse had started about her.

Asking the question is important, but it's only part of the *H* in H.E.L.P. How you attend to the answer can reinforce or undermine the person's feelings of connectedness and competence.

Giving the Gift of Complete Attention

When we ask the question, it is important to use the warm, open, and attentive body language we described earlier. We may want to add the person's name to the question: "Jane, what is happening in your life?" There are several reasons for this.

A person's name is usually one of the most beautiful sounds in the language. In childhood the people closest to us and those who cared the most called us by name. Strangers couldn't. People who didn't care never learned our name. So, using a person's name is a wonderful way to connect with children of all ages.

Most of us think three or four times faster than people talk. This tempts us. All too often we jump to conclusions, prepare a response, and interrupt the speaker. This is especially true when we are with children or adults who are upset, because they take more time to gather their thoughts. As people who want to help, we are not alone when it comes to interrupting.

Medical patients in America have an average of eighteen seconds to talk before the doctor interrupts. It's no surprise that one study found about half the doctor-patient interactions led to misunderstandings. Fortunately, if we don't have the time to hear the response to the first question in H.E.L.P., we don't have to ask it.

Great leaders know how important it is to listen. Norman Rockwell was not yet a famous illustrator when he met General Eisenhower, but years later he wrote, "What I remember most . . . was the way he gave me all his attention. He was listening to me and talking to me, just as if he hadn't a care in the world, hadn't been through the trials of a political convention and wasn't on the brink of a presidential campaign."

Giving someone our full attention doesn't mean we let the person drone on endlessly. If we do, our minds will wander and our body language will no longer communicate interest in the other person. People are likely to feel disconnected and incompetent. In fact, unless the crisis is the death of a loved one that generates shock and denial, it's best to respect privacy and avoid intimate details by moving right on to the next step in H.E.L.P.

The purpose of asking someone under stress to share their hologram is not to get lost in what happened but to invite that person to find a slightly different, less stressful view of the event.

9

Naming That Emotion

"A friend is someone who halves your sorrow and doubles your joy."

—AUTHOR UNKNOWN

When Judy, the mother of a sixteen-and-a-half-year-old, and a participant in one of our two-session workshops, described the difficult time she was having with her daughter, Jenny, we asked her what was happening. Jenny hadn't made her bed or picked up her room in weeks. In addition she'd recently started to talk back to her parents at every opportunity. Judy had asked Jenny repeatedly if anything was bothering her. The response was always a loud no, followed by the stomping of Jenny's feet and the slamming of her door.

Judy's husband, John, responded to Judy's complaints by yelling at Jenny to clean up her room. When that didn't work and Jenny snapped back, "You can't make me," he stormed out of the house and then refused to discuss the problem any further.

We asked Judy how this made her feel. After some thought she said that she felt as though she was living in a combat zone. She admitted that she often felt attacked when Jenny screamed at her or John complained about Jenny's behavior. We asked her if she would role-play a typical situation using one of the "agree-or-set-free" disarming techniques that we taught earlier that night. Judy chose to role-play a dinner scene at home using a setting-free approach. A participant who was a college student and just a little older than Jennifer volunteered to take her role.

When Judy asked, "What's happening?" and the student mumbled, "Nothing," Judy said, "I've noticed that you haven't been talking much to us lately. It seems like you might need some space right now. If that's true, I just want you to know that's okay with us, as long as you are safe. You're not in any danger, are you?" The student answered no. Judy waited and then responded, "Whenever you don't need as much space, I want you to know that we're here to listen, and I promise nothing will ever get worse by talking about it with us."

The student felt that Jenny would respond well to this and suggested that Judy try it. The next week Judy was pleased to report that things were better. Jenny finally felt free enough to tell her mother that she had been fighting with her best friend and was so involved that she had missed the tryouts for the school play. Judy felt relieved that it was less serious than she had thought.

It's Not What's Happening but How It Affects Us

Let's say that we used a disarming approach on a stressed-out person and it worked. Then we asked the H question and now we've found out what happened to get them all stressed-out. Perhaps we're comforted, like Judy, because we don't think it's serious. Or maybe we're relieved, since they're not upset because of something that we've said or done. Perhaps we just want to get on with work or get back to play. Maybe we inquired about what happened and now can easily explain it or apologize. On the other hand, we may have faced a sim-

ilar situation and may want to share how we got through it or
tell the person how to solve the problem.

All of these are very natural responses, but they offer less
than optimal support to the stressed-out person. Why?

Given how rewarding strong social support could be to that
stressed-out person, let's start with how each potential response is likely to undermine support. Remember the two *C*s
of caring support: connectedness and competence. If we try to
quickly dismiss the problem as minor, apologize for our role,
or abruptly return to work or play, we will undermine the
other person's sense of connectedness. If we talk about our
own experience to explain or solve the problem, we will undermine the person's sense of competence.

Without genuine support the person will probably remain
stressed-out and continue to disrupt our lives by attacking,
withdrawing, or becoming immobilized. In addition we will
not enjoy the rewards of creating a caring place to live or
work.

Going Beyond What Happened

By constructing more of the hologram we can take advantage of opportunities for much more insight and far more support than the typical responses described above. Learning only
what's happened is like looking at a black-and-white photo-
graph. Asking the person how it made them feel adds the richness and abundance of color to both our understanding and
our relationship.

Imagine that you are visiting your favorite amusement park.
The sun is warm and there is a gentle breeze carrying the
shouts and laughter of children. Two people on the roller-
coaster ride catch your eye. The shoulders of one rider are
hiked up, almost touching his ears, his eyes are shut, and his
knuckles are white. The other rider is grinning, waving his
arms wildly and shouting gleefully with each plunge. As much

as the first rider can't wait to get off, the other can't wait to get back in line for another turn.

On life's roller coaster it's not what's happening but how we feel about the ride. The same event can evoke very different emotional responses.

Divorce, usually a painful ending of a marital relationship, can be a wrenching earthquake for some, a welcome relief for others, merely the acknowledgment of a long-standing emotional separation for still others, or perhaps even a vindictive windfall for a few.

Emotions Put People into Motion

We are moved by our experiences and the feelings they evoke. Our emotions are reactions to our interpretation of what is happening to us. These feelings often simmer and spill over into other places and relationships. Someone who is stressed-out may not even know what he or she is feeling. Stressed-out people who are unaware of their feelings are just upset, preoccupied, and difficult to live or work with. Even if they know that they are angry, upset, or overloaded, they may be unable to do anything about it. Those feelings of helplessness may trigger feelings of depression.

Depression is an emotion that can put people into slow motion. Deep depression can totally immobilize. When we get to an impasse with someone and feel stuck, it's important to remember that sharing emotions can get people and relationships moving again.

Unrecognized Emotions Interfere with Living Life Fully

When people are feeling intense emotions, it can be as if they are possessed. Like Jennifer they may seem distant, and so involved in their internal struggles that they are not fully available for other interactions. For Jennifer, her feelings were interfering with her ability to relate both at home and at school.

Unexpressed Emotions Affect Our Health

Suppressing an emotion requires active mental effort. It's draining. Researchers led by James Pennebaker, Ph.D., at Southern Methodist University used coroner reports to contact a group of people one year after their spouses had died either in auto accidents or by committing suicide. Studies have shown that the sudden death of a spouse ranks highest in stress-related life changes that can be detrimental to one's health. Those widows and widowers who kept their grief to themselves reported the most illness. In fact the group that shared their feelings with others showed no significant increase in health problems. Suppressing emotions seems to lower our immune system's resistance to disease.

In another study Dr. Pennebaker's team measured the physical responses of volunteers who had been prepared to tell an experimenter about upsetting events in their lives. Instead some volunteers were first asked to talk about a trivial event. The monitors showed their bodies to be under considerable stress. When these volunteers later talked about their troubles, some sobbed and trembled, but their bodies then relaxed deeply. It was as though a burden had been lifted.

In a related study Dr. Pennebaker demonstrated that volunteers who simply wrote about personal traumas for as little as fifteen minutes a session over four consecutive nights made fewer visits to doctors during the next half year than those writing about trivial matters. In another of these studies, students who used writing to express their feelings about major traumas earned higher grades the next semester than students who were not given the opportunity to do so.

People Don't Know Their Emotions on a First-Name Basis

Feelings often put people in motion without ever being recognized. In many homes, such as Jennifer's, people don't talk a lot about their emotions, and certain emotions are never acknowledged. The feelings are acted upon or acted out in indirect ways, but they are not discussed openly and directly. In Jennifer's family it was as if there was a sign over the front door that read, THOU SHALT NOT BE ANGRY.

Some people are fortunate to have been raised in families where it was okay to have and express all kinds of feelings, including negative ones. They are generally comfortable with their own emotions and have no need to keep them out of awareness. They are lucky because when feelings are not felt, labeled, or talked about, they are more scary and disruptive than they need to be. Unexpressed or unaccepted feelings put our bodies and minds at risk. When we do not express or accept our own feelings, they can seriously undermine our sense of well-being. This is why asking people what they are feeling can be so supportive. Our concerned questions can validate their feelings and bring us closer to them.

E Is for Emotion or Effect

Once it's clear what's happening, we recommend asking, "How does that make you feel?" or "How do you feel about that?" About half the time the person will answer with an emotion, such as "mad," "sad," or "glad." This is great. He has added color to the hologram and you can move right on to the next step in H.E.L.P. The other half of the time we may need to repeat the question because the person tells us what he thinks instead of how he feels about the event. If we still do not get an emotion, we may want to imagine what we would feel in their situation and gently inquire if they feel that way. Or we may move right on to the next step in H.E.L.P.

Most of us can discriminate between words describing emotions and those describing facts, but it often helps to review lists of such words so that we can more precisely label our feelings. This will help us to feel more in control and to communicate more clearly. Here is a basic list to review. It is meant to be read through slowly. Careful and repeated study is particularly helpful for those of us who don't tend to share our feelings with others. Comfort with the list enhances emotional vocabulary. We could offer a longer list, and many exist.

Taking time to read the list now will show us that these words are more effective and less judgmental than many other words we could use in the next step of H.E.L.P.

HAPPY	SAD	ANGRY	HURT	AFRAID
Committed	Ashamed	Annoyed	Abandoned	Anxious
Determined	Blue	Bitter	Deceived	Bashful
Excited	Defeated	Bored	Embarrassed	Doubtful
Fantastic	Depressed	Bothered	Empty	Frightened
Good	Disappointed	Confused	Foolish	Intimidated
Grateful	Down	Enraged	Left Out	Overextended
Great	Embarrassed	Impatient	Lonely	Powerless
Optimistic	Empty	Infuriated	Needy	Pressured
Passionate	Hopeless	Irritated	Pained	Scared
Pleased	Miserable	Mad	Tired	Suspicious
Relieved	Sorry	Resentful	Tortured	Uncertain
Surprised	Tired	Trapped		Upset
Thrilled	Worthless			Weak
				Worried

Remember Judy? When she later asked Jennifer how she was feeling about missing the tryout, Jennifer pushed her away a little by answering, "There'll be other plays." Judy then masterfully applied the first part of the agree-or-set-free technique. She asked again by agreeing, "Yes, there will be other plays, but how did missing the tryout make you feel?" Jennifer's eyes began tearing up as she talked about her disappointment. She so much wanted to be part of the cast. She also expressed how lonely she felt.

Alternatives to "How Do You Feel About That?"

Some workshop participants have a hard time imagining themselves asking, "How are you feeling about that?" or "How does that make you feel?" As we mentioned in the introduction, many men in our culture have difficulty connecting with people on an emotional level, and some think that focusing on feelings implies a lack of strength. Also, asking about feelings in some formal situations might create problems for anyone. The alternative we recommend is the question, "What Effect is this having on you?" This accomplishes many of the same objectives as our standard question. Another alternative might be, "What's it been like for you?" Many people prefer the first alternative because the E in Effect is part of the acronym H.E.L.P.

Those who share our preference for the standard question and are looking to improve their ability to recall it quickly in difficult situations may find useful this comment from one of our participants. He explained that he simply took the bottom, horizontal "foot" off the E to get the F in Feeling.

If feelings are a little foreign to your everyday style of relating, we would still encourage you to use the word feel. Try it first on yourself, then with your family, and finally with other stressed-out people in your life. It may be new and awkward at first. Take the risk. Life is an adventure. You'll be pleasantly surprised at the rewards.

Once Labeled, No Longer Possessed

When we get sick, most of us try to find out what is wrong with us. If we can't figure it out, we may ask our family. If the family is stumped, we may go to the pharmacist or the doctor.

There are two main reasons that we search for answers and go to doctors. The first is pain. The second is fear.

If we know what is causing the pain, we can usually find something for relief. If we know what is wrong, we can usually stop worrying about it.

Research shows most people feel better when the physician makes a diagnosis and gives the symptoms a name. After all, if there is a name for the problem, it makes it seem more controllable. Others have experienced it. There may be a cure or a way to alleviate the symptoms. We are no longer dealing with the unknown. The diagnosis makes us feel a part of the human race again. We feel connected to all the other people who have ever had the symptom. Our situation does not seem as much out of control. This makes us feel better even when the symptoms are basically the same and we are still in pain.

Everything we just wrote about disease can be applied to emotional states. Oftentimes one of the most helpful things we can do for ourselves or another person who is upset is to define the emotion. Most people feel better when they can identify an emotional state and give it a name.

Once an emotion is recognized and labeled, it no longer possesses us. We possess it. We no longer feel alone. We know many other people have shared the feeling, or there wouldn't be a word to describe it. We no longer feel incompetent. After all, others have felt the same way and survived. If we are on tilt, we are more likely to regain our balance. Remember, the first step in stress management is to recognize the stress and identify the source. The first step in dealing with emotions is to recognize the feelings and label them.

Emotions Are Not Cast in Concrete

Most people go through a series of feelings in response to an event. Early studies of death and dying suggested that the terminally ill went through five stages. These were the denial of shock, the anger of "why me?", the wishful thinking of bargaining, the depression of hopeless resignation, and finally the comfort of acceptance. Any major loss was expected to evoke the same stages. We now know that some of these feelings may never be experienced, those that are experienced may follow a different pattern, and some may be felt more than once. Often people cycle through stages of anger, sadness, and guilt.

People's emotional responses to any event can be expected to change as the feelings are recognized, felt, and expressed over time. Thus if the situation evoked by the first question in H.E.L.P. is unchanged, we cannot assume the answer to the second question has remained the same. It is usually best to ask the second question more than once.

Expressing our feelings helps us to manage our emotional state in a variety of ways. Many people are not aware of their emotions and find it hard to get in touch with them. Without encouragement they may get stuck in the same place. Focusing on their current emotion encourages them to move on to other emotions, thoughts, and plans. This is why so many people say, "Hey, you've got to get in touch with your feelings."

Once recognized, feelings are no longer an obstacle to change or communication. Instead emotions can become a wonderful bridge between two personal "places" or two people, as we will see in the next chapter.

10

Listening Actively

"The greatest gift we can give
is rapt attention to one another's experience."
—AUTHOR UNKNOWN

Barbara, a biology teacher who recently retired to the Adirondack Mountains, was visiting her sister, Jackie, in New York City. As they walked out to the street, the bright lights, towering buildings, belligerent horns, and foul exhaust fumes wrapped around them.

The two sisters walked quickly to the corner. While they waited for the light to change, Barbara declared, "Listen to that sparrow." Jackie looked at her in amazement and asked, "How could you hear a sparrow in the middle of all this?"

Without a word Barbara took the subway token Jackie had given her earlier and flipped it into the air. As the coin clinked on the sidewalk, a dozen heads turned in the same direction.

Barbara smiled and whispered to Jackie, "We hear what we listen for."

Hearing Is Not Listening

Fortunately, listening to a person under stress is not as difficult as hearing a sparrow's chirp in the city.

When a person shares something and we ask how he or she feels about it, however, we need to listen actively. We hear with our ears, but we listen with our eyes, our minds, and our hearts.

When Jennifer told her mother, Judy, that she'd missed the tryouts for the school play, Judy heard the words. What Judy listened to, however, were her own needs, as a caring mother, to protect her daughter. As a result, she temporarily missed Jennifer's pain. Once Judy asked Jennifer how she felt, she heard about her anger and her loneliness.

The next step would be for Judy to let Jennifer know that she heard more than her daughter's words. Judy needed to let Jennifer know that she is aware of the situation as Jennifer saw it and her pain as she felt it. With this kind of support Jennifer could feel more connected and competent.

Judy told us that she turned to Jennifer and said quietly, "It looks like you're feeling angry and lonely about missing the tryouts." This demonstrated to Jennifer that Judy had listened and really heard. Notice that Judy reflected back both what Jennifer felt and what had happened with equal clarity, simplicity, and objectivity. Judy avoided adding any other agenda. She might have criticized Jennifer's inaction or her strong feelings, but these would have been Judy's issues and they would have undermined Jennifer's self-esteem. This accepting, nonjudgmental reflection is called active listening.

In "It Looks like you are feeling ____ about ____ ," the first blank represents the emotion, the second represents what's happening. In active listening the light is focused on the other person. That's the "you" in the sentence.

The L step is a statement, but we must remember that meaningful support is given by asking questions and listening, not by explaining or advising.

We Think Faster Than People Speak

In a demanding world it is not easy to put aside our own thoughts, feelings, and judgments. In order to listen actively, we have to put forth effort and keep an open mind. And an open mind is not an empty mind. We think faster than we hear, so, while we are listening, our minds may be flashing back to what the person said happened or racing ahead to what we are going to say next.

Active listening is a skill that requires interest and concentration. In order to really hear another, we pay attention to what he or she is saying. Paying attention means that we ready ourselves for the task of receiving his or her communication. The *in* in *interest* relates to the direction that our attention and thoughts need to take. We need to direct our awareness toward the experience of the other person, or we will be unable to reflect it back accurately.

When we concentrate on listening, we are taking an action that makes the other person the sole object of our attention. We prepare ourselves for surprises by suspending preconceptions and shutting out all other distractions, to the best of our ability.

Concentration is also required to distill the essence of the situation and the other person's reaction. All this takes effort, but it's worth it. Our attention, interest, and concentration are gifts we give the other person. These gifts are delivered by our body language and our accuracy in reflecting what we hear.

Give the Gift of Listening Without Taking on the Problem

When we are performing the *L* step, we need to connect without becoming overinvolved or overwhelmed. When people crawl into painful shells or attack us, as Jennifer did, the normal boundaries and communication patterns change. If this happens at work, the changes can be very disruptive. Remember what happened to Sally and Mr. Jackson when his brother was arrested for selling cocaine. Mr. Jackson sought too much nurturance from a relationship that wasn't created to meet his temporary, but overwhelming dependency needs. Sally wanted to extend her hand but ended up getting pulled into quicksand. Unlike the stranger on an airplane Sally needed to maintain boundaries in an ongoing relationship.

By moving quickly from "What's happening?" to "How are you feeling about that?" Sally would have protected both of them. In addition she would have listened more fully to his feelings because her mind would not have flashed back to his brother's AIDS, his mother's mental illness, and his marital conflicts. These problems would have remained his and not become hers.

Empathy, Not Sympathy

Active listening communicates that you have heard and understood the person. This is empathy, not sympathy. Sympathy involves sharing common feelings, as Sally did with Mr. Jackson and we do at funerals, where we may cry with the bereaved. Unfortunately pity as well as compassion are forms of sympathy, and sympathy is often emotionally draining.

Empathy, on the other hand, involves imagining how we would feel if we could step into the other person's life space and see the world through his or her eyes. Fortunately it is liberating because we quickly come out again to share our understandings.

An actor identifies and becomes one with the feelings and character portrayed, but empathy requires two—one to give and the other to receive. Thus empathy frees us from the burden of sympathy and prevents any loss of identity.

If people could always tell us their feelings, we could just insert their words into the blanks in the L step. Perhaps we could restate what they said in our own words, in order not to sound like a parrot, but it would be fairly easy. Of course if people were in touch with their feelings, they might not be withdrawing or attacking, and we might not need to give them our support. Most of the time active listening requires tuning in with active empathy to help people identify and label their feelings.

To get on the same wavelength, we can try to figure out their feelings from their body language, or we can ask ourselves, *Given this situation, how might this person feel?* Sometimes it can be helpful to check within ourselves and ask, *How would this situation make me feel?* Unfortunately this can be dangerous. Putting ourselves into the situation can become just another filter that prevents us from appreciating the uniqueness of the other person's reaction.

If we are trying to help a person who seems unable to tell us about his experience, we may need to offer words that might describe his feelings. Regardless of our approach, we must check back with the person to find out if we have truly and fully understood him. Our goal is to feed back only what we think the person meant and felt, nothing more and nothing less.

Being Totally Present to Present the Gift

When people do not listen with empathy, they usually do one of two things. As Deborah Tannen, Ph.D., points out in *You Just Don't Understand*, men usually try to fix the problem and women usually try to sympathize by sharing their own experience. Since many things can't be "fixed" and doing so usually undermines the person's sense of competence, men are often given the advice "Just be there for her" or "Just listen to her."

The word *just* underestimates both the effort involved and the value of these activities. Our presence can be an extraordinary gift. However, "being there" can be an energy-consuming activity. "Listening" also means maintaining the focus on the other person by "not talking" about our own experience. "Not talking" also takes tremendous energy.

We have mentioned a number of obstacles to being there that H.E.L.P. addresses, including feeling overwhelmed, not knowing what to say, and attending to our own agenda. The system also helps us to overcome fears of making things worse, inviting overdependency, and disrupting boundaries. By using it we also avoid many typical but unhelpful responses. These include warnings, sermons, advice, lectures, judgments, labels, interpretations, interrogations, and superficial reassurances.

A Mother Is Fully There for Her Son

Jane demonstrated the value of open, active listening with Billy, her shy seven-year-old. He always had a difficult time doing his homework and then seemed reluctant to play outside until he had spent some additional time at home with her. Lately he had stayed indoors, following her about almost every afternoon.

A few days after Jane attended our workshop, Billy was tearful and upset when he came home from school. When Jane asked, "What's happening?", Billy sobbed, "Mrs. Crawley yelled at me." Jane was about to tell him he shouldn't be upset, ask him how he had gotten in trouble again, and explain that his teacher was only trying to keep the class under control. But this time she caught herself and remained open to what could unfold if she listened.

Jane thought H.E.L.P. and, after asking Billy how that made him feel, she warmly reflected how upset he seemed to be about Mrs. Crawley yelling at him. In this way Jane avoided making her son feel inept and lonely. Instead she had validated Billy's feelings and made him feel both accepted and connected in a more healthy way. She reported that after their talk Billy was able to settle down to homework faster and then couldn't wait to go out to the park.

Accepting the Person in Spite of the Behavior

What if someone tells us that he has done something wrong and shows no remorse when we ask him how he feels? As a parent Jane must help Billy learn right from wrong. Most adults, however, resent other people who take the role of critical parents toward them. At the same time, many people want to be honest when they hear about wrongdoings and immediately criticize the person.

In reality, whatever someone does is the best thing that that person can do. It may be illegal, immoral, and even harmful, but it is the best the person can do at that moment to adapt to the world as he or she sees it.

We do not have to accept behavior that we believe to be wrong, but it is important to accept the person. Such acceptance usually leads to better behavior, as we will explain in later chapters.

Watch Your Expectations

In addition to providing a clear structure for what we are going to say next, the *L* step in the H.E.L.P. system keeps our minds from racing ahead and frees us up to listen completely to the person's feelings. In this way we are more likely to avoid denying, interpreting, disagreeing, judging, or overidentifying with the person's situation or feelings. The fear and pain described will not become our fear or pain. Also, when we give the person our undivided interest, we are less likely to become bored, rush the other person, or let our minds wander.

It is critically important to approach each situation as though it were totally new. Our own experience and expectations predispose us to judge and compare whatever we hear against what we already know. This automatic process becomes a filter that distorts our ability to hear accurately.

In Buddhism there is a concept of "beginner's mind," which

relates to a way of approaching any experience as though it were for the very first time. Beginner's mind allows you to appreciate the uniqueness of the moment and the uniqueness of an individual. So it is important for us to try to hear just what is being said and to let go of expecting to hear either specific reactions we've heard before or how we think we would have reacted to the situation.

Other Filters

Besides our own experience other factors can distort our ability to hear another person accurately. If we are tired, hungry, or emotionally upset ourselves, this physiological state becomes a filter that garbles the message. Deciding that the event is not important, that the other person is overreacting, or that the person will feel better in the morning prevents us from hearing their pain or discouragement. Making a judgment that the person has misinterpreted the situation or that she is not telling the whole truth also prevents us from hearing her concerns. Finally, there are cultural differences, both in perception and in expression that can get in the way of our communications.

Please don't let all this be discouraging. Our hope is to provide inspiration for approaching other people with the intention of really listening in a new way. When we pay attention, become interested, and concentrate, new learnings emerge that overcome the distance between people. Being heard is such a rare event that everyone appreciates any attempt made to really listen.

Letting Them Know You're Listening

By reflecting back what we have heard, we provide direct evidence that we gave the other person our undivided attention. The words "Looks like . . ." makes it clear that we don't claim to *know* how he or she feels, we are only guessing. With-

out such a disclaimer our empathy might sound like an accusation and be met with "You can't possibly know what I feel!"

A few other good disclaimers are:

"It sounds like you're feeling . . ."
"I get the impression that you are feeling . . ."
"I have a hunch that you are feeling . . ."
"It seems to me you are feeling . . ."
"Is it possible that you are feeling . . ."

We chose "Looks like . . ." to keep the H.E.L.P. acronym,
since we use the word *listen* as our cue. Each of the other disclaimers work equally well. It is important for each of us to
find one we like so that it will sound natural.

Some people use questions as disclaimers, such as "Are you
feeling . . . ?" or "Could you be feeling . . . ?" We don't like
these, because questions can more easily be misinterpreted as
accusations. When we want to use a question, we can try "Are
you saying that you feel . . . ?" Whatever our approach, it is
important to keep our responses tentative. This gives the other
person room to modify his or her reaction.

Missing the Mark

If people disagree with the feelings we offered them
through empathy, we can apologize, ask again how it makes
them feel, and then complete the *L* step. Another option is to
reflect that it seems they have mixed feelings or that they are
confused. This is true for many people. Some people do know
how they feel but have a hard time expressing it. Happily
there is now a major and growing industry publishing personal
cards to help us express our deepest emotions.

When people seem unsure of their feelings and their body
language says that they are hurting, it is empathic to say, "I
can see that it's hard for you to talk about your feelings," or
"I can see that this is uncomfortable for you to talk about." En-

couraged and supported by our understanding, the person will usually react by visibly relaxing.

Once we have given the gift of listening, we can invite people to share their plans with us. As we will discuss in the next chapter, by allowing them to make their own plans, they will feel competent as well as connected. In so doing we have offered true friendship in a time of need. This sort of support is important because, as a wise person once said, "We arrive in this world alone, we depart alone. This time called life was meant to share."

11

Planning Is Empowering

*"Each of us can see only one small slice of reality, so
how can we possibly know what's right for others?"*
—AUTHOR UNKNOWN

When we left Larry and his editor, Susan, he had disarmed her attack, explained that he'd called a repairman for
the copier, and asked warmly, "You seemed really upset, is
there anything else bothering you?" This was a powerful question because it included both an empathic reflection of feelings and an open invitation to tell him what's happened in
Susan's life. Larry used this question to start the H.E.L.P. and
Support that he wanted to offer her.

Susan respected the way Larry had avoided a fight without
putting her down. She wanted his continued support and felt
comfortable enough to let Larry know what was going on in
her life. Susan motioned him to come into her office. Behind
the closed door Susan explained that her husband had forgotten to mail the tax return before his business trip, her son was
sick, and her back-up sitter for day care was not only out of
town but hadn't left her the name of a substitute.

Larry responded, "Boy, you've got a lot of problems there. What bothers you the most?"

"My son is with a new neighbor, and I'm worried and feeling guilty."

"Looks like you're juggling a lot of responsibilities at home and you're feeling really bad about not being there for your son when he's sick."

Susan sighed, saying, "I'm sorry I jumped down your throat. I should have known you hadn't forgotten."

"That's okay," Larry said, and then after a pause, he asked, "So, what are your plans?"

"I haven't figured anything out, but maybe I could call the neighbor and find out how things are going. I guess I could always go home if I had to."

"Sounds like you've got some good options for a tough situation. I'll certainly do everything I can to hold down the fort here," Larry added as he got up to leave.

The Importance of Suspending Judgment

Before Larry could start providing H.E.L.P. and Support, he needed to disarm Susan's criticism. Her attack was completely out of character. Something had to be going on. By suspending judgment and not taking things personally, Larry had avoided defending, denying, counterattacking, or withdrawing.

In Chapter 3 we described the caring way Larry dissipated Susan's anger by agreeing and moving with it. After that he could ask her about what was going on in order to find out what was happening. Then by asking Susan how she was feeling about the most troublesome event, he helped her clarify her emotional responses. By listening actively and reflecting those feelings in an understanding way, he helped Susan to feel both competent and connected.

When Larry asked, "So, what are your plans?" he invited Susan to sort through her options. In this way, he avoided taking any undue responsibility for her problems while conveying his belief in her competence. Larry also expressed his goodwill in spite of her attack by offering to cover for her should she need to leave. People on tilt experience this kind of offer as a powerful source of reassurance and support.

Many people might want to jump in to give Susan some advice or tell her their worst child-care war story. Giving her advice presumes that Susan needs advice. It also implies that Larry has more insight into what she needs than she does and that she wants him to give her advice.

These implications accompany any unsolicited advice we give, not just the advice an assistant might give a boss. Giving advice usually undermines the person's self-confidence. Unfortunately this happens when the person most needs self-confidence.

Even after Susan considered her options and told Larry her plans, Larry continued to suspend his judgment, resist offering suggestions, and maintain his support. As long as Susan's response did not put anyone in danger, Larry chose to support her self-esteem by accepting her plans. If Susan wanted some practical suggestions, she could have asked for them. Since she didn't, Larry moved right on to make a supportive statement, a reassuring promise, and a nonverbal close by getting up to go.

Sometimes Plan Just for a Day

There is often a temptation to ask the stressed person to figure out why the situation happened and how to keep it from ever happening again. Doing either might have met some of Larry's needs, but Susan could easily feel burdened, belittled, and controlled. After all, Larry is not her father, and even most fathers would recognize how this might undermine a daughter's confidence.

Larry's goal is emotional first aid, not counseling. Asking about plans helps to focus people in the "here and now" rather than the past, which cannot be changed, or the future, which might seem overwhelming. The question also mobilizes people to look at what has to be done. It gets people off tilt. Once plans are made and the short-term problems feel under control, people can make much better long-term plans to prevent future problems.

Our Advice: Don't Give It

By avoiding advice we avoid not only malpractice of the mouth but many other problems as well. We don't have to get defensive about our suggestions if we haven't given any. We don't have to feel powerless and frustrated when the person we're giving advice responds repeatedly with "Yes, but ..." We don't have to risk trying to talk others out of their feelings or imposing our value system. More important we avoid the "one up, one down" positions of ourselves as "helper" and others as "the helped"; ourselves as "adviser" and others as "advisees"; and ourselves as "counselor" and others as "clients."

If we think of ourselves in any of the "one up" roles, we send a diminishing and destructive message to the other person to get into a matching "one down" role. The more we think of ourselves as separate, strong, and active, the more we may unintentionally cause others to see themselves as alone, weak, and passive. Thus giving advice endangers the sense of connectedness and competence people receive from real support.

It's Got to Be Theirs

By asking, "What are your plans?" we are activating the other person. We're keeping the ball in his or her hands, rather than grabbing it away to give advice. We are communicating things about both the problem and the person. We're saying, "This is a situation that can be lived with and out of which order can be made. I respect you as a capable person with ideas and I want to spend time with you to help you sort out your ideas about this situation." With that sort of message most people in most situations will respond actively and enthusiastically. The question also helps those who are more impulsive and may have made a snap decision. It invites them to take time and consider other options.

When Larry asked Susan this question, she answered, "I haven't figured anything out, but maybe I could call the neighbor and find out how things are going. I guess I could always go home if I had to."

It is unclear whether Susan had thought of these solutions either before or during the discussion. It really doesn't matter. She now feels more in control of the situation. Talking about her concern helped her to organize her thoughts, recognize possibilities, and come up with solutions.

If the person doesn't respond, we might try saying, "I can see this is hard for you, do you want to talk about plans?" If he answers no, he may not be ready to plan. People are ready when they are ready, not when we are. Often they may be overwhelmed by their emotions, and as we will discuss later, it may be best to give them permission to stay with their feelings. Most situations do not require instant action or an immediate response. Upon reflection we find that those situations that are truly important are rarely urgent and those that are most urgent are rarely important in the long run.

If the person gives us a plan but doesn't seem to like it, we can ask if she wants to consider other options. We might say, "That is a possibility, but you seem uncomfortable with it. Would you like to bounce some ideas around together? Maybe we can come up with some other ways to handle the situation." Asking permission to look at options together is important. It clarifies who owns the problem and that we have neither a predetermined solution nor a need to control the outcome. It also communicates our belief that there are options.

Milgram's Diabolical Experiments

Psychologist Stanley Milgram began a fascinating series of experiments about obedience at Yale in the 1960s. In the first experiment Milgram told men that he was studying the effects of punishment on learning. He then divided them into "teachers" and "learners." Milgram instructed the teacher to punish the learner if he made any mistakes while he memorized a list of word pairs in another room.

The men in the teacher group sat in front of an impressive machine with thirty switches indicating levels of shock from 15 to 450 volts, with graded labels from "Slight Shock" at the low end, to "Danger: Severe Shock" and "XXX" at the high end. Unbeknownst to the "teachers," the machine was a fake and the learner was an actor. As the actor made mistakes and the shock level increased, he started pounding on the wall. Finally he stopped responding entirely, as if unconscious. If the teacher hesitated, Milgram told him sternly, "Whether the learner likes it or not, you must go on until he has learned all the word pairs correctly. So please go on." The results? Almost 65 percent of the men obeyed to the very end.

One of Milgram's later studies involved only a very small addition to the orders, but it made a big difference. When the experimenter added, "You have no choice," almost all the teachers stopped. Many said that of course they had a choice, they could leave. And they did. It seemed that just mentioning the word *choice* alerted them to the fact that there were options.

There Are Always Options

People who regret making a serious mistake during a difficult time in their lives will often say that it never occurred to them that there were any other options. There are always options. Even if we were completely paralyzed and couldn't *do* anything, we could change our *view* of things.

Many people don't know there are always options, and under stress it is easily forgotten. This is why we recommend asking, "What are your plans?" If the person has no plans or has only one plan, the question encourages a search for possibilities rather than the single best answer.

Brainstorming

Most people get stuck in problem solving because they begin evaluating options as soon as they think of them. This tends to block the creative process. A technique called brainstorming separates the invention of possibilities from the evaluation of solutions. It encourages the playful exploration of a situation and its potential opportunities rather than a grim look at a problem and its ultimately flawed solutions.

To apply this while H.E.L.Ping people, just ask them if they would like to brainstorm solutions with you, explain how it works if they ask, and begin the process. When the inevitable evaluations come up, quickly compliment their critical thinking and then ask them to hold off evaluating solutions until they've got more options. Once several choices have been generated, people can usually sort them out and pick the best available alternative based on their values.

In this business of making and evaluating plans the customer is always right. What if we think they are about to make a mistake? Remember that good judgment comes from experience, and experience often comes from bad judgment. We must resist the urge to give advice and we must let others make their own decisions.

Nothing gives more support more effectively or more quickly than a carefully worded question. We've suggested some of the best questions we know. As James Thurber wrote, "It's better to know some of the questions than all of the answers."

The Dummy Dance for Dangerous Plans

If the solution they've picked is potentially dangerous or could really backfire, they may be under too much pressure to think clearly. We must not argue. Concrete thinking hardens under pressure. This kind of thinking is a symptom that there are strong emotions involved. It is often good to switch back to listening or to try doing a "dummy dance." We might do best to act dumb—it isn't hard for most of us—and say, "I don't know much about that, could you tell me more?" or "I'm confused, can you run that by me again?"

What if the dummy dance not only doesn't work but the person seems "dead" set on destruction and we are very concerned about some truly dire consequences? First we need to remember that we've already H.E.L.P.ed the person by listening and by slowing the process down. When people calm down, they often reconsider decisions they made when really upset. We can try to slow the process down further by suggesting, "Let's talk more about this tomorrow."

If we think they are about to harm someone, it's time to call the police or a suicide hot line. If we think the situation is serious but not immediately dangerous, and our relationship is strong, we might suggest their getting professional counseling. In Chapter 26 we discuss ways to make referrals work.

P Is for Permission

Often when people are in great emotional distress, they are just not ready to make any plans, but they still need our help. The second option for the P in H.E.L.P. involves giving them permission to have upsetting feelings and not to do anything about them. We do this by passive listening and being there for them. Our silent presence communicates acceptance loudly.

It isn't so easy to "just listen." It's far easier to interrogate, interpret, and give advice. What makes it so difficult to be there and listen? Other people's pain scares us and we want it to stop. Pain is not the enemy; the real enemy is our fear. Why else do we want to instantly cheer up other people or ask them to do something with us to get their minds off the problem? Acknowledging and accepting our fear can help us to do the same for others.

For most of us the words *pain* and *suffering* have become synonymous. We assume that people are suffering because they are in emotional pain. Most of the time the pain is part of the healing, and tears are a release on the road to resolution.

How comfortable are you with tears? Let's use tears as an example to help overcome whatever discomfort intense, emotional situations evoke in us. Permitting someone to cry may be particularly difficult if we deny ourselves this uniquely human response.

Did you know that over 90 percent of women and 50 percent of men cry at least once a month and that these people tend to enjoy better physical and emotional health? People cry when they are sad, but also when they are happy, angry, anxious, or afraid. In addition the chemistry of emotional tears is different from those due to other stimuli, such as smelling onions. The protein content is highest in emotional tears and appears to help rid the body of harmful stress-related chemicals. Both tears and laughter are natural, stress-reducing responses.

When someone looks like he or she is about to cry, we can get out some tissues and wait. We don't have to say anything. There are no one-liners to take away the pain. People don't need to be free of their emotions, they need to experience them fully so that they can move on.

How can we tell them that we have heard their pain, that it hasn't overwhelmed us, and that we'll be there when they are ready to move on? We can look at them caringly and say, "This must be very painful for you," or, "I can understand your feelings given the situation."

Jenny and Judy in the Next Act of H.E.L.P.

When people are on tilt, they are often incapable of coming up with any kind of plan, let alone seeing multiple options. Unless they are sitting on train tracks in front of an oncoming engine, one of the greatest gifts that we can give others is this permission to be where they are and feel what they are feel-ing. If they are emotionally stuck, we can let them know that feeling stuck and doing nothing is totally appropriate given the situation. Paradoxically this acceptance and permission usually liberates those who are stuck.

After Jenny confessed to Judy that she had missed the try-outs for the school play and Judy listened to how angry and lonely Jenny felt because she couldn't get a part in the play, Judy asked Jenny whether she had any plans. Jenny replied bitterly, "What do you mean, plans? It's over. The cast is set, and I can't be part of it." Judy gave her a hug and said, "I can see that you feel very angry and discouraged. You really wanted to be involved in the school play, and now there is no way that you can do that."

As Jenny looked at Judy, she stopped frowning and her eyes widened. Then Jenny began to smile. "Yes," she announced softly. "Yes, there is a way that I can be part of the play. I can join the crew," she explained quickly as her voice got stronger, "Maybe do props or even be the stage manager. Oh, thank you, Mom, thank you. What a good idea." Judy smiled, and said, "But honey, it's your idea?" After they hugged again, Judy said, "I'm so proud of you."

Often when we give people permission to be stuck, to hurt, even to be discouraged, it gets them off tilt and enables them to come up with a plan. Letting people know that we accept them, just the way they are, is the essence of healthy support. In the next chapter we will explore this kind of Support, the final step in doing what H.E.L.P.S.

12

Giving Support
by Affirming Their Uniqueness

*Only through accepting and celebrating differences
can everyone feel competent and connected.*

Joe's day at the office had been flooded by waves of feelings
and thoughts about the last angry words he'd exchanged with
his wife, Kathy. Twenty-one years of marriage . . . Coffee with
Bill had been good, and his offer of tennis sounded like just
what he needed, but he wondered if he would have to cancel
out. He was exhausted from all the sleep he'd lost. As Joe
drove home, he started to regret putting off those three overdue accounts still another day. What would he say if his boss
got on his case on Friday?

As Joe turned the key to unlock his back door, he could hear
the frenzied scramble of paws on the floor. When Joe pushed
the door open, Travis, his Irish setter, jumped up on him and
licked his hand. *Travis is always happy to see me,* Joe thought
before grabbing his leash so that they could take their nightly
walk.

The Pet Prescription?

Having a pet is not only a pleasant distraction; research has shown it enhances people's health, just like other forms of social support. One year after having a heart attack pet owners are more likely to be alive than those without pets. Another study found that even after stressful events, dog owners visit doctors less often than people without pets. In still another study, over a ten-month period, seventy-one adults who acquired pets reported significant improvements in their physical and psychological well-being. The presence of a friendly dog has even been shown to lower people's blood pressure and heart rate.

What do these studies of four-legged friends have to with our giving support to stressed-out people? Should we buy them pets? No, but maybe we can learn some important lessons.

With a grant from the National Institutes of Health, Karen Allen, Ph.D., and her associates at SUNY Buffalo studied forty-five professional women while they performed mental arithmetic in the presence of their dog, their best friend, or neither. You guessed it—with their pets the women's physical responses remained close to normal, but with friends their stress responses soared. Dr. Allen credits the results to the evaluative and judgmental tendencies of human friends.

You Are Exactly Where You Need to Be

When people are stressed-out and on tilt, the strong feelings they experience make them feel out of control and isolated. The persistent loving attention of their pet is affirming and reassuring. They're okay, no matter what they've done, and they will not be abandoned, no matter what has happened. A pet's unquestioning acceptance inspires the owner's increased acceptance of both self and pet.

Can't we do as well or better? Social support consists of the things we say to give people positive information about themselves and their relationship with us, as well as the things we do to help ease their burdens. If we listen sensitively and reflect accurately the happenings, feelings, and plans of people on tilt, we validate them. Our questions and reflections demonstrate our caring involvement.

We can also add words that convey some of the unconditional acceptance that makes pets so special. The words we find most effective for this kind of support are very simple: "It sounds like you are doing the best you can with a difficult situation." Finally, we can ask if there is anything we can do to help. In this way we can extend to them the physical assistance they may need without undermining their sense of competence.

Unfortunately most of us have trouble resisting the moralizing tendencies that pets avoid so naturally. Pets cannot interrogate, interpret, advise, lecture, preach, judge, criticize, or shame. Pets simply accept us and the world.

The Self-Help in Other-Help: Genuine Acceptance

Fortunately in the course of trying to accept others, we can identify issues that trouble us and learn to accept ourselves more fully. Only by respecting and accepting ourselves and others can we set the stage for healthy relationships and personal growth.

When we suggest telling people, "It sounds like you are doing the best you can with a difficult situation," are we asking you to lie? We might be if the words read ". . . the best anyone can . . . ," but that's not what we are inviting you to say. Every one of us is doing the best we can, as we see it at any moment. If we could do better, we would. Put another way, even if people are planning or doing things you wouldn't do, it's important to recognize that if they could plan or do better, they would, but they can't, so they don't. Besides, if everyone were like us and did what we would do in their situations, the world would be a very boring place.

People on tilt need our affirmation. This doesn't mean we have to like everything they say or do, but if we can separate their current behavior from their personhood, we can continue to accept them and their unique human potential.

By examining our reactions to what others are planning and doing, we can enhance our own personal growth. If we are upset by a person's situation, irritated by a person's feelings, or threatened by a person's plan, it may help to remember what Carl Jung said: "Everything that irritates us about others can lead us to an understanding of ourselves." We need to ask, "What is this situation or person telling me about myself or my life about which I am uncomfortable?" The answers to these questions will give us precious insight. This allows us to make some changes in our own behavior or in our expectations for ourselves.

If the person's situation seems precarious, it helps to remember that times of crisis involve both danger and opportunity. As one executive said, "The time I grew the most is the time I spent hanging on by my fingernails." After all, as Admiral "Bull" Halsey said, "There are no great men in this world, only great challenges which ordinary men rise to meet." Even if the person's plan seems unwise, in time, he or she may choose to change it. If not, we've found that people generally learn the most from their mistakes.

This philosophy of acceptance can give us the detachment to affirm other people, their situations, their feelings, and their plans rather than warning, judging, advising, or even praising them. Essentially it allows us to celebrate each person's uniqueness and give them the gift of support.

Empathy Revisited

Later that week Bill called Joe to see when they could play tennis. Joe's voice sounded anxious when he answered the phone, so Bill thought H.E.L.P. and asked, "What's happening?" Joe hesitated, but replied, "I'm really getting behind and I'm worried about getting some heat about it." Bill realized that he could skip *E* since Joe had already said how he felt. Going right on to *L*, Bill reflected, "Looks like you're backed up and afraid your boss isn't going to cut you any slack. How do you plan to handle it?"

There was a pause, and then Joe thought out loud, "I guess I'm thinking of letting him know I'm behind, but I don't think I can tell him about Kathy yet." Bill waited and avoided making any suggestions, but responded, "I can understand that." Joe seemed relieved as he said, "Well, maybe I'll just tell him I'm having some personal problems." Bill didn't think that would be disastrous, so he felt impatient to nail down a time, call for a court, and get back to work. Then he remembered how Support can be used to keep things brief and said, "Sounds like you're doing the best you can with a tough situation."

After a few seconds Bill followed up with, "By the way, how's eight o'clock on Saturday for tennis?" and Joe said, "Yeah, sounds great, can you get us a court?" "I'll give it a try and get back to you," Bill said as he hung up the phone.

Bill was pleased with the results of giving Joe H.E.L.P. and Support. By calling, Bill had connected with Joe. By listening actively, Bill had invited Joe to sort through what was going on and his feelings about it. When Bill reflected what Joe had said, the backlog of work and his anxiety about it sounded just a little different to Joe, and he got a better understanding of his reluctance to tell the boss what was going on. When Bill helped Joe to get in touch with his feelings and his needs, Joe was able to solve his own problem and increase his sense of control. Thus Bill's call helped Joe feel both more connected and more competent.

Bill got on Joe's wavelength by listening with openness and understanding. This is empathy, and empathy is the foundation of giving people support.

Do Women Have More Empathy Than Men?

Research with children shows that boys are just as skilled as girls when asked to take another child's point of view or to imagine what someone is feeling. So where does the stereotype that women are more empathic come from? Do women develop more empathy as they grow up?

There is no question that empathy can be learned. If you've read this far, you have probably increased your empathy. Studies suggest that women usually read body language a little better than men, but the differences are quite small. In addition a review of more than one hundred studies concluded that investigations based on self-report questionnaires reported large sex differences in empathy, whereas those using other measures found "little evidence of a sex difference in physiological response to another's emotional distress." Could it be that the sex stereotype comes from women just describing themselves as more empathic than men?

An important piece of this puzzle comes from a Harvard study of undergraduates who were asked to report their feelings and those of a partner while one taught the other how to do something. The results? Women and men were equally empathic, but those in the student's role were more tuned in to the teacher's feelings than the other way around. Maybe it's all a power issue. Workers, privates, and Indians have far more to risk by failing to pick up emotional signals from their bosses, officers, and chiefs than vice versa. Until recently women have taken more subordinate roles and thus may appear more "naturally" empathic, but clearly both men and women can learn empathy and can offer it as support to others. It really comes down to deciding that this change is important.

Focusing on Strengths

When on tilt we lose sight of the rewarding aspects of our lives and our positive personal qualities. Instead we focus on the overwhelming problems we face and the impossible people in our lives. We become discouraged. When another person recognizes this and empathizes with us, it is affirming. When reminded that we have overcome similar situations in the past, it is empowering.

When friends and family testify from personal experience that they have seen us handle difficult problems in positive ways—that we have insight, patience, stamina, and other sterling qualities—we feel more competent.

Every person we encounter has overcome a myriad of large and small crises, losses, and disappointments. They have survived. We can honestly tell them, "Things are tough, but you're a survivor."

We may need to point out the person's strengths more than once. A good alternative is "You seem discouraged now, but I've seen you do a lot to help yourself over the years." It is supportive to reflect that the person has the characteristics of a survivor.

Brief Is Better

When Bill called back the next day to let Joe know that he'd reserved the court, Joe told him that he had spoken with his boss and had found him to be understanding. Bill said, "Good for you!" Joe thanked him for making the reservations, but then sounded like he was back in the dumps when he complained that his car was in the shop. Bill said, "Sounds like you're having a string of bad luck. I've always been impressed with the way that you manage to survive the worst and keep moving. Let me know if there's anything I can do to help." Joe answered, "I don't think that will be necessary, but I'll call you if I need a ride. See you at eight."

Notice that all Bill's empathic and supportive responses have been short but powerful. He focused on what Joe had done to help himself, but he also acknowledged Joe's misfortune. Bill didn't belabor the bad news, but moved right on to focus on Joe's strengths. Then he offered to help. Each response is powerful in its brevity. In addition, by keeping things brief, Bill can keep in touch and connect with Joe frequently during this difficult time in his life.

Some people in our workshops ask if giving H.E.L.P. and Support repeatedly is a good idea. For our needs as learners there is no question. We know that it takes dozens of conscious repetitions of a new skill to replace an old habit and make the new one automatic. So repetition is not only good but necessary for our ability to give H.E.L.P. and Support.

Won't we get exactly the same responses? Almost never. About the only thing we can count on in this life is change. As the ancient wise man Heraclitus said, "You can't step into the same river twice." Will it sound canned? Not if you are truly listening.

Both of the authors have received H.E.L.P. and Support repeatedly from our students, co-workers, and family members without recognizing or resenting it. Later people have smiled and fessed up to it, but, like most people, we need to connect when we're stressed-out. So give H.E.L.P. and give it often to people on tilt.

Healthy support, even for major crises, can be and should be brief and cumulative. Small increments can add up to make major differences in the person's overall experience of a crisis. After any crisis there are ripple effects that put people on tilt repeatedly. If we are going to be there for people over time, it's best to avoid marathon sessions. This way they can call on us more often without feeling that they are burdening us, and we can avoid burning out. This affirms the relationship and increases their sense of connectedness.

There is another important benefit to brevity. If we spend hours instead of minutes, we imply that their problem is enormous and/or that they are incapable of handling it. This undermines their self-confidence and breeds unhealthy dependency. By doing what H.E.L.P.S. briefly and repeatedly, we can affirm both their sense of connectedness and their sense of competence.

Pediatricians who are studying nighttime crying patterns to help babies and parents sleep better are learning that briefer is better. By asking 122 mothers of nine-month-olds about their babies' sleep patterns, researchers found that rocking babies to sleep may double the likelihood of their crying during the night.

Babies normally wake up in the middle of the night, but rocking, holding, feeding, singing, or walking babies to sleep seems to teach them that they can't go to sleep on their own. Once babies can sleep through the night without food, parents are now advised to leave the room while their children are still awake, to return only to offer brief reassurances without picking them up, and to tuck them in with special toys or blankets to comfort them when they wake up later on. Although other research shows that it's hard to spoil a baby with too much love and attention during the day, there are times when briefer is better, even for babies.

Bill also gave Joe another kind of support when he said, "Let me know if there's anything I can do to help." People on tilt often need a helping hand. If Joe seemed overwhelmed by everyday tasks and Bill had the time, he could have made sure that Joe took his support seriously by asking, "Is there anything specific I can do for you today?" By indicating a willingness to help out, Bill again affirmed the relationship. By asking rather than taking over the tasks, he affirmed Joe's ability to handle things. This added another dimension to the support he gave Joe. When Joe's car was still in the shop on Saturday, Bill's offer helped Joe feel comfortable enough to ask Bill for transportation to the courts and afterward to the shop to pick up his car.

Time to Practice

Do you feel ready to give H.E.L.P. and Support to stressed-out people? Our guess is that you do and you don't, depending on the circumstances. In an ideal situation, with time to think, it'd be a cinch. All you'd have to do is ask, "What's happening?" followed by, "How does that make you feel?", reflect back what you heard to let them know you'd listened, and then ask if they have a plan or give them permission to flow without one.

Then what's the problem? When you most need the technique, you, too, will be under stress. Research has shown convincingly that when people are under pressure, it becomes much more difficult to access new skills.

The solution? Practice H.E.L.P. often enough that it becomes automatic. Then and only then, stressed-out or not, we will be able to apply our new learning in any situation where it is needed. Of course we must also manage our own stress well enough to realize that the other person needs H.E.L.P.

Happily there is an ideal way to practice giving H.E.L.P. and to manage our own stress at the same time. As we go through our day, we can repeatedly ask ourselves the same sequence of questions and listen to our answers. This will increase our self-awareness, reduce our stress, and prepare us to H.E.L.P. others.

By H.E.L.P.ing ourselves before trying to H.E.L.P. others, we will gain the skill and confidence we need to cope effectively with stressed-out people. As we continue to practice giving H.E.L.P. and Support to others, we will increase not only their competence and connectedness but our own as well.

The next section focuses on developing our self-H.E.L.P. skills.

PART III

THE IMPORTANCE OF H.E.L.P.ing YOURSELF

13

Self-H.E.L.P.

"So long as we cannot accept what we are at any given moment of our existence . . . we cannot change."

—NATHANIEL BRANDEN

Sharon's work as a computer programmer and consultant exposed her to a wide range of people, from computer fanatics to computer phobics. Still she just wasn't prepared when Leonard, an executive, leaped up and began pacing back and forth across the office just when she was explaining a special application of a new program.

Sharon had almost completed a contract with a major corporation, when the CEO had insisted that she teach Leonard how to use the program. The CEO thought this would better prepare Leonard to supervise the program's implementation in his division.

Shaken by Leonard's intense pacing, Sharon tried to figure out what was happening. She really hadn't a clue about what was going on with Leonard. Tuning in to her own feelings, she recognized that she was confused and frightened. That seemed like a reasonable reaction to Leonard's unusual behavior. She knew that she had almost no time to plan something to say or do.

Having gone through H.E.L.P. for herself, she wanted to connect with Leonard in a calm, supportive way, but to her surprise she blurted out, "Are you angry with me?"

Leonard stopped pacing. He looked at her. Then he smiled, shook his head, and said, "No, why would I be angry with you? I've got sixteen other things on my mind. I find it really hard to concentrate when I have more pressing priorities. Besides, computers are not my best thing. I wish S.J. hadn't dumped this on me at this time." Reluctantly he sat down again.

Stress: You've Got to See It to Manage It

Sharon had recognized and coped with a very stressful situation in two ways. She did so first by acknowledging the stress within herself as well as within Leonard and second by giving H.E.L.P. and Support to herself before trying to connect with Leonard. No, Sharon did not follow the approach perfectly, but like many other powerful tools it still worked, which is all that matters in this imperfect world of ours.

For most of her life Sharon tended to ignore feelings in herself and others. In many ways computer programming suited her precise, logical mind, and her programming spoke for itself. She left the large company where she'd been for five years and began successfully to market her consulting services. For the past several years she had been creating special programs for a major corporation and training personnel at different sites to use them. The direct interface with people was exciting, but often the encounters became tense. Sharon recognized her need to acquire new skills for stress management and took a workshop.

Now, when Leonard started pacing, her rapid heartbeats told her that she had perceived danger and wanted to flee. Sharon became aware of the tightness in her muscles and of her racing mind. She acknowledged her stress and decided to do some of the belly breathing she'd learned. Focusing on the in and the out of her breathing, she slowed not only her breathing but her heart rate as well. By controlling her breathing Sharon was able to take the edge off her stress response, but she still needed to stop the disorganized, repetitive, and negative thoughts going through her head. It was time for some self-H.E.L.P.

Do Unto Yourself Before You Do Unto Others

Self-H.E.L.P. has many benefits. First it is critical to calm ourselves before doing anything to cope with others. If we are not relaxed and centered, our anxiety and imbalance can become contagious and can escalate the stress of the encounter. On the other hand the warmth of our calm, quiet focus can evoke the same in others when we H.E.L.P. them.

Executives asked to identify critical events in their careers consistently chose as the most damaging to their advancement situations where they had acted out of anger. Self-H.E.L.P. is a powerful way to use anger as a signal for prudent and constructive action rather than impulsive and destructive reactions. The greatest remedy for anger is delay, and self-H.E.L.P. offers a productive pause in any interaction.

By using H.E.L.P. on ourselves we also get to know how it feels to be H.E.L.P.ed. This makes our H.E.L.P. even more empathic. In addition, when we take care of ourselves first, we are in a better condition to respond to others.

There is another important reason for applying self-H.E.L.P. first. Unless we count ourselves among those who need H.E.L.P. at times of stress, we place ourselves above others. This false attempt at establishing competence only distances us from others and prevents true connectedness.

Finally, applying self-H.E.L.P. frequently during the course of a day enhances the details of our lives, clarifies our reactions, and helps us to develop a calmer, more effective process of daily living. It creates small pauses for experiencing and thinking that prevent thoughtless and automatic reactions. By regularly using self-H.E.L.P. we develop a more aware and hence a richer way of being in the world.

H: Ask Yourself, "What's _Happening_?"

The first step in self-H.E.L.P. is to detach ourselves from what we think we saw. Jumping to conclusions, taking things personally, and making mountains out of molehills are such automatic responses that these phrases have become overused, even for clichés.

We are never impartial observers. We give meaning to everything we see and hear. This meaning reflects both what most people in our culture generally think and the unique things we think based on our individual experiences. This is why it is easy to overlook our distortions. We need to step back and look at events through new eyes.

One of the best ways to do this is to try to observe the situation the way a news reporter or an anthropologist might and then to delete all adjectives and personal opinions from our description of it. Another way is to imagine putting ourselves on the moon and looking at what happened from a distant perspective.

All of us constantly tell ourselves stories about what we are experiencing, what we have experienced, and what we are going to experience. Stories like "I'm really messing this up," "I've never been able to do things right," and "Everyone will know I'm stupid" provide a running commentary about the events of the day. These stories are based on our experiences as we remember them, but they often have little to do with what actually happened.

Our stories are very important because they color whatever we experience. They are not only about ourselves but about others as well. Stories will almost always distort what we see others do, what we think they think, and what we feel they are feeling. That's why it's so important to step back and try to be objective.

As soon as she became aware that she was stressed-out, Sharon tried to resist the urge to tell herself that she must have done something to upset Leonard. She delayed long enough to ask herself what was happening. She needed to describe the event and give herself "the facts, ma'am, just the facts."

Sharon thought in a neutral way, *While I was right in the middle of showing him how to key in this report, Leonard leaped up. He looks angry and is pacing back and forth while I'm still sitting here. He hasn't said anything. I haven't seen this before.*

E: Ask Yourself, "How Am I Feeling?"

As discussed earlier, most people are not in touch with their emotions, or at least those emotions that were considered "wrong" in their family of origin. "Wrong" emotions are usually avoided, denied, or repressed because they generate anxiety. For some of us those are dangerous ones, such as anger; for others they have to do with weakness or neediness. Fear itself may be the forbidden feeling in the person raised to replace fright with false bravado.

Even if we are comfortable feeling our emotions, most of the time we are so busy thinking and telling ourselves stories about what is happening and what is going to happen, that we do not take time to get in touch with our feelings. Labeling feelings is the first step in managing our reactions. When Sharon asked herself, "How am I feeling?" she knew she felt scared. Searching for another split second, she also recognized feelings of responsibility and confusion.

L: Listen to Yourself

At times our emotions get separated from our perceptions. We just feel rotten or edgy or miserable and we don't know why. Our minds race ahead, creating dire consequences, or they speculate about judgments that other people may be making. These details may liven up our stories, but it is more effective to focus on how we feel in response to what actually happened. By listening to our commentary as we reflect on the *actual* situation, we center ourselves and stop our racing thoughts.

Filling in the blanks of "I feel ____ about ____" may seem like belaboring the obvious or too simple to be of use, but most people are surprised by what it can yield.

Sharon might have thought, *I feel scared, somehow responsible, but confused about Leonard's unexplained pacing.* Then she would have realized that she was jumping to the assumption that Leonard was angry with her. As it was, Sharon recognized that she felt scared because Leonard looked angry as he was pacing, and given his behavior, she was unable to continue the work that she had been assigned.

Or Make a List, But Keep It Short

Besides rapid breathing and tense muscles, racing thoughts are a clear indication that we are in a stressful situation. Sometimes it is hard to focus on the H.E.L.P. sequence mentally because our brains continue automatically replaying similar insults and injuries past, present, and future. The more we tell ourselves these stories, the worse we feel. This is a good time to grab the closest scrap of paper and jot down the letters *H, E, L,* and *P.* By doing so we have already begun interfering with the swirling spiral of negative thoughts.

Next we quickly write a phrase or two after each letter. Sometimes a couple of words will do. Next to *P* for *Plan,* for example, we could just put "flow," "breathe," "ask questions," or "delay." Writing things down clarifies what we see and feel. A later chapter about personal journals explains more about this process and its many benefits.

The difference between writing in a journal and what we are recommending here involves immediacy and brevity. We need to think quickly and respond appropriately to the current situation. We can't wait for a regular journaling time, nor can we afford the luxury of detail. Brief is better.

The goal is to understand what we are feeling in response to what is happening. Summarizing our reactions in a clear sentence or two has an amazing effect. We know where we stand and we can respond more effectively. It puts us back in control. In addition to reducing stress, it is a rewarding way to practice the active-listening skills so essential to H.E.L.Ping other people.

P: *Plan Your Possibilities*

Sharon had successfully used self-H.E.L.P. and was about to ask Leonard what was happening, but his continued pacing intimidated her. Instinctively she blurted out, "Are you angry with me?"

No harm was done in this case, and the problem was resolved quickly. Nevertheless jumping to assumptions about events or other people's emotional responses is risky. Voicing your conclusion, even in the form of a question, might lead to an unnecessary counterattack or withdrawal.

By asking, "Are you angry with me?" Sharon skipped from her self-H.E.L.P. into the *E* in the part of H.E.L.P. she gave Leonard. She didn't ask what was happening. However, once Leonard was questioned about a feeling that he was not experiencing, he became aware of his preoccupation with other matters and enacted a plan (*P*) to return to the work at hand.

The power in both of the H.E.L.P. techniques comes from the effectiveness of what each letter represents. Neither other-H.E.L.P. nor self-H.E.L.P. depends on perfect execution or exact sequence. They are simply tools for making meaningful connections within ourselves and with other stressed-out people.

Moving Forward by Stepping Back

When Patty's son had called from college asking if he could bring a girlfriend home for the weekend, Patty said it would be fine, but she was surprised by her discomfort. Patty used self-H.E.L.P. to sort through her many feelings, clarify her concerns, and plan what to say on the phone when she called him back.

By recognizing her excitement about seeing her son and her fears that he wanted to sleep with his girlfriend in her home, Patty realized three things. First, that she had made a big assumption, second that she needed more information about his request, and third that she needed to formulate a house rule. Patty decided to call him back to express her excitement about his visit, ask what sleeping arrangements he envisioned, and if necessary, state her rule about separate quarters.

S: Self-acceptance

Just as others are always doing the best they can with whatever situation they face, we are always doing the best we can with each situation we face. No matter what we have done, if we could have done better, we would have, but since we couldn't, we didn't.

Volumes have been written about self-acceptance. Unconditional acceptance by our parents would probably have taught us to accept ourselves unconditionally. Since most of us were raised by human parents, we need to supplement the unconditional and counteract the conditional acceptance we received.

By adding the S of support to H.E.L.P. and getting H.E.L.P.S., we can remember to give ourselves the Support we need with affirmations such as "I'm doing the best I can" or "I'm making progress." Any time we think we've made a mistake and our plan has failed, we can remind ourselves that no one was ever born goof-proof and that so far we are all still human.

Mistakes also provide new information, and we can use this information to make better plans. Thomas Edison never failed when he was looking for the right filament for his electric bulbs. Why? Because, as he put it, "I didn't fail, I found ten thousand ways that didn't work." Think of what could be gained if we considered every mistake to be a potential solution to another problem.

It is said that in school we learn a lesson and take a test, but in life we take a test and learn a lesson. Whatever the outcome of a plan or action, we can be assured of learning something if we choose to be open to the lessons of life. When we are supportive and gentle with ourselves, the learning involves less pain and more joy.

Practice on Your Own Time

Self-H.E.L.P. and Support is a wonderful way to grow and a great way to practice what we hope to do for others when they are stressed-out. We recommend using the self-H.E.L.P. method at least several times a day for a week or two before applying other-H.E.L.P.

By practicing the approach on our own time, we can avoid using it on others prematurely and undermining their sense of competence and connectedness. We can develop the habit of tuning in to ourselves by using H.E.L.P. at regular times during the day. At the same time, as we learned from Sharon's experience, we don't need to follow the approach completely or to do it perfectly in order to be helpful.

14

Disarming
and Redirecting Attackers

"An attack is often a cry for understanding."
—AUTHOR UNKNOWN

Each morning we awaken to great opportunities. Some involve our dreams and goals; others come disguised as problems and stressed-out people.

Edith, a lively, dark-eyed woman, began her first day, as an adjuster at an insurance company, by looking for her new office. The directions from the receptionist led her to a small, double-sized room containing two desks, several chairs, and a divider leaning against the far wall. Paper mountains covered every desk, cabinet, and table in the room. *Doesn't look like I'm expected,* Edith thought. The question, "Are you the new adjuster?" startled her.

Turning, Edith saw a tense-jawed, handsome man of medium build with raven-black hair. The voice was deep, the accent Hispanic. He seemed rushed. "Sorry about the mess, but I've got a lot to do today. We won't have time to talk, but my name's Johnny. Nothing personal, but I've never had to share an office before. I tell you, I'm less than pleased. They didn't give me much notice either."

Tempted to snap back with one of her habitual, put-him-in-his-place remarks, she slowly took a deep breath into her graceful, petite frame. Last weekend's workshop taught her to yield and to ask questions when attacked by people on tilt. "It's a pleasure to meet you, my name is Edith. You seem in a hurry. Which desk is mine?"

"I'll take the one by the window," Johnny replied. "You can push my stuff off the other one and make yourself at home. Gotta run." Edith didn't like his attitude. She felt dismissed and she didn't like the idea of having to move his things. Taking his view of it, though, she knew that facing a new office mate, without much warning or any choice must have been stressful.

After a night of sleepless thoughts about starting a new job, Edith knew she was tired. Fortunately she recognized the value of flowing with events when she knew that she was not at her best. Tempted to fight and assert herself with Johnny, she kept hearing the workshop's message:

"When under attack, breathe slow,
avoid 'no,' and redirect the flow."

Edith had prepared herself to slow down and be open to anything today. This confrontation was a little more than she had anticipated, but she had avoided the sort of response that had gotten her in trouble before. Edith found Johnny appealing, in a strange way, and hoped the office dilemma could be resolved without alienating him.

She could see that the advanced skills she'd learned for coping and negotiating with demanding, stressed-out people were going to pay off.

Anticipating Attacks

One of the best ways to flow is to assume that each experience in life has a purpose; we can learn from the stressed-out people and problems that come into our lives. Edith had changed jobs to grow professionally but also to present herself in a new way, to new people, in a new setting. When we live or work with people who have known us over time, their crystallized expectations inhibit changes. Our growth can be threatening to others. After all, change is inherently stressful.

In her last job Edith succeeded by working harder than anyone else. Unfortunately she also isolated herself by fighting or fleeing whenever she was attacked by stressed-out co-workers. Now she was determined to change that behavior.

Psychological Sunburn

When people get burned by fiery bosses, heated arguments, and blazing deadlines, it's as if their skin is sunburned. They blister at new stimuli. It's best to learn about their most burning issues and then let them cool down before doing anything else together.

Interpersonal friction needs lubrication. It's up to you to supply the suntan lotion. If other people had the balm themselves, they would already have used it to avoid or treat their sunburn. If you're also on tilt, wait for them to ease the heat.

Edith's friendly response did not solve the office problem. Lacking both time with Johnny and personal energy, Edith waited. She was pleased with her reaction to a touchy situation.

Difficult People or Difficult Places?

Work is like a second home. Relationships can become difficult, but calling people bullies, snipers, stonewallers, whiners, or worse is sure to backfire. Tense people launch attacks. Retaliations risk escalations.

Is there a formula to measure work-site stress? Yes. Tension at work is the sum of each worker's stress, multiplied by the intolerance each person has for intimacy, divided by the square footage of available office space, the height of the partitions, and the number of windows.

To arrive at each worker's stress level, calculate his or her living and commuting tension. Take the anxiety at home, subtract the support available, divide by the number of rooms and doors in the house, and multiply by the discrepancy in personal needs for privacy.

If this stress index is starting to sound like mumbo jumbo, you're catching on. No one knows enough to predict co-worker stress. But all of us can prepare ourselves, and even benefit from it.

Relaxing Our Body, Preparing Our Mind

Insanity is doing the same thing over and over again and expecting the outcome to be different. We chuckle at that definition, because most of us operate that way, at least some of the time. Every day we look for a perfect day, on our terms, in an imperfect world that we cannot control. And yet we're surprised and get upset when things don't go our way.

Instead of anticipating stress and stressed-out people, we prefer to deny reality. This creates an illusion of peace and tranquillity, but it doesn't prepare us to handle stress or other people in productive ways.

Are there better ways of coping with stressed-out people? Certainly. But first we have to remember to manage our own stress. By relaxing repeatedly throughout the day with deep belly breathing or a favorite alternative, we can become more receptive to what life brings us. We can become more curious and open to what we can learn, without concern about the final form of the lesson.

The inability to predict the future can be scary or exciting, depending on how we look at it. If Edith had expected to find what she had found in her last job, she would have re-created it. Instead she relaxed and prepared for an adventure with new people and events.

The First Person to Get Mad Has the Right of Way

The next time a stressed-out person crosses your life's path, breathe slowly from your stomach area and allow yourself to relax. Find out where the person is headed, yield the right of way, and avoid a collision.

How can you do that? First of all, avoid saying no to stressed-out people. Recognize that their capabilities and their experience of the world are limited by their state of arousal. If they need to back up, withdraw, or leave, as mentioned earlier, simply agree and set them free.

Yielding to Johnny, however, doesn't mean Edith gives in to cleaning up his mess. This would be equally self-defeating.

Another part of yielding is removing obstacles to learning opportunities. Differences of opinion, for example, are not only inevitable, they can be productive. If you and your boss always agree, your mind is unnecessary and there is no need to communicate. Diversity is a rich source of solutions.

Edith decided to flow with the situation and use verbal aikido. First she acknowledged Johnny's legitimate feelings and avoided become defensive. She sidestepped his attack and, shortly, we'll see how she turned him around.

Slowing Down on Black Ice and Maintaining Your Composure

The importance of slowing things down when attacked cannot be overemphasized. Yes, there are deadlines, but most are only guidelines. Few *dead*lines are worth risking a relationship, no less a life to meet.

Recently one of us encountered a phenomenon of the north called black ice while rushing through the rain to pick up his children on time. In seconds rapidly dropping temperatures had frozen the rain on the road into a thin, treacherous layer of invisible ice on the blacktop surface. Cars slid in all directions, some out of control, like a group of first-time ice-skaters.

What had been ruthless freeway driving slowed to a cooperative crawl. There was a common danger. It came from the elements and affected everyone. The only way to minimize hurt to oneself was to look out for the other guy. The bent and bruised fenders would fill body shops for months to come, but when it was possible, people yielded the right of way graciously. They tried to get out of each other's way and waited their turns patiently. Later they had fun sharing stories with their friends about what had happened. Wouldn't it be nice if we didn't need black ice to see that "there is more to life than increasing its speed"?

How Animals Disarm and Avoid Violence

When fights are about to break out among animals of the same species, there are ritual ways of negotiating to prevent bloodshed at all costs. Carl Sagan and Ann Druyan report that in captive chimp colonies when the males arm themselves with stones, the females pry their fingers open. If two quarreling males ignore each other, another chimp, usually a female, will playfully pull them together.

When macaque monkeys from Japan were fed only if they pulled a chain to electrically shock another macaque, 87 percent preferred an empty stomach. One monkey starved for two weeks rather than cause pain to another. How soon will we, as human beings, start living up to these standards?

Want to see five acts of human violence an hour? Watch prime-time television. Want to see twenty-five? Watch an hour of cartoons.

Unfortunately our "art" both reflects and affects our lives. As

Sagan and Druyan write, "We live at a moment when our re-lationships to each other, and to all the other beings with whom we share this planet, are up for grabs."

We do have a choice. Our lives depend on it. We can disarm the world, one by one, interaction by interaction, and day by day. By treating other people in new ways we can make and keep the peace.

Ben Franklin's Diplomacy

When Thomas Jefferson became the American minister to France, he followed in some very big footprints. Jefferson al-ways denied being Benjamin Franklin's replacement. He would only acknowledge succeeding the great diplomat, since no one could replace him.

Jefferson was often asked to explain the secret of Franklin's diplomatic brilliance. His response? Jefferson said that he had never heard of a single encounter in which Ben Franklin di-rectly contradicted another person. Franklin avoided saying no consistently and brilliantly.

Preventing the Suicide Hour at Home

If you have young children, you probably know about the suicide hour. It's the last sixty minutes before dinner. You're making the meal while the children are asking for permission to do what *everyone* else is doing, or playing too loudly with three friends who are equally hungry, or refusing to do any-thing that must be done before dinner, or enacting all of these unpleasantries at the same time.

As one of the dishes you are making in the midst of this bedlam begins to burn, your spouse enters, tells you it's been a rough day at work, and asks why you look so frazzled.

What's the recipe for suicide prevention? It'd be nice if, like the mother in the *Family Circle* cartoon, you could call out, "I'm it for a game of 'hide and go seek,' " and then see everyone scatter to leave you in peace as you scrape out the burned pot.

That's great reframing, but you can only fool kids once. Instead you can redirect the flow at five P.M. by inviting the guests to leave and closing the permission center for the hour. Then make it clear that no one eats till what needs to be done is done, and the more people help, the sooner everyone will eat. Does this work? Better than most alternatives to the suicide hour, including homicide!

Fighting Before *the Vacation*

Tina, an energetic retiree, shared with us some hard-earned wisdom about her family's vacation stress. She had found that family members automatically used a variety of tools to maintain domestic peace, such as privacy behind closed doors, and distancing through daily activities. But when they were on vacation together and had to face forced proximity, they resorted to other, less constructive devices.

Like most families brave enough to vacation together as adults, a fight erupted regularly on the second or third day of any car travel. That was before Tina discovered how to disarm her family.

Two days in advance of a trip to California Tina asked everyone at the dinner table if they'd like to start fighting now or schedule it for the first day of the trip. That way, she explained to them, they could get the traditional vacation fight behind them early. Following a riotous recounting of war stories from vacations past, the prevacation fight became a family joke, and travel has been easier ever since.

Redirect Attacks on You as Attacks on Problems

Johnny was surprised when he came into the office the next day and saw nothing on Edith's desk. She had carefully moved each pile of papers onto the floor in front of the desk by the window.

"Well, I can see you're already starting to take over the place," Johnny challenged. "I'm sure it seems that way," Edith responded. "I really hate crowding you. I also didn't want to interfere with your filing system, so I kept all the piles intact." Johnny looked across the room and said, "I wonder where you'll want to put the divider now."

A moment passed as Edith collected her thoughts. At the workshop the message was to ask about the principles and the process instead of arguing for or against the positions taken by stressed-out people. Johnny looked glum. Edith offered, "Shall we decide together how we want to position the divider?"

"I guess so," Johnny responded. They spent a half hour re-arranging the furniture, finding the best place for the divider, and even ordering a potted plant to soften the effect. An extra filing cabinet provided a new home for Johnny's paper piles. Edith was delighted by the results. The office looked nice, but she was even more pleased by the cooperative effort that had infused the process. Her attitude and communication skills had prevented what could have been a messy fight. *What a good way to start a working relationship*, she thought to herself. *And I got to yes by avoiding no and by redirecting the flow.*

Beyond Assertiveness

In the 1970s two psychologists, Robert Alberti and Michael Emmons, started the assertiveness movement. A breakthrough at the time, assertiveness has its limitations with stressed-out people. "I" messages may avoid accusations and bring respect, but they can also create distance and undermine the other person's sense of competence. The "broken record" technique of rephrasing what we hear and repeating what we want is most useful in situations where our rights are clear, we don't know the person, and we don't want an ongoing relationship.

On the other hand, when a relationship is important and ongoing, it becomes crucial to explore the process by which the two of us can flow. Optimally a relationship is a dance in which we take turns leading and following. By responding to another's needs we show that we care about the other person. We reflect how much we value his or her ideas for finding a mutually beneficial solution.

After all, if the solution is not fair, both of us lose. It is likely that the one who makes the greatest compromise won't adhere to the agreement or will want more than is fair next time, to compensate for the earlier loss.

Making Lemonade?

One of the keys to negotiating the flow is to avoid an investment in any one solution. It is important to wait until we know each other's needs before we jump to the assumption that the other person wants what we want. Often there are solutions in our differences.

Two sisters wanted the same last lemon. They could just have decided to split it, but neither was pleased with that solution, and a sour fight was in the making.

By slowing down the process and asking why each needed the lemon they learned that one wanted the peel to flavor some icing for a cake while the other wanted the juice of the lemon for a pie. You guessed it; by avoiding no they found yes and danced happily, most of the time, ever after.

The University of Life

By mindfully and intentionally focusing on the process of our moment-to-moment experience, each event can present an opportunity for growth. This approach of seeing what lessons we can learn from what life brings us may seem "soft" and foreign, particularly in the work setting. If we read the great business leaders, however, it's clear that they use it.

The hard-nosed turn-around artist Lee Iacocca summed it up when he referred to challenges he'd met so creatively:

> "We are continually faced by great opportunities brilliantly disguised as insoluble problems."

What a healthy way to walk through life. In the next chapter we'll learn another healthy way to bring us still closer to those we care about at home and at work.

15

The H.E.A.L.T.H.Y. Way

"All that we send into the lives of others comes back into our own."

—EDWIN MARKHAM

When we asked people to share what happened to them since the last class session, Edith stood up quickly. "The only way I've ever handled stressed-out people in my life is to 'drop out.' I just stop listening to everything they're going through. Growing up in my family, that's what I did to protect myself."

Pausing only to catch a breath, she continued, "As you all know, I used disarming at work a couple of weeks ago. The way we divided the office space and desks is really working out. Last week I used H.E.L.P. to keep my beautician from spilling her whole life story. She's a great hairdresser, but I was getting spaced-out listening to her chatter. We both felt better after I ran through H.E.L.P. and gave her some support. It makes it a lot easier to stop talking without being rude."

Everyone was silent. Robin, the woman sitting next to Edith, smiled. "I had much the same experience, growing up and all," she said. "But what do you do when you're living or working with someone who's *always* stressed-out? I'm talking about my sister. Her life is always a disaster, and she's depended on me since we were kids. Her neediness drives me crazy. But I'm the older one and she's always counted on me."

Robin knew that changing lifetime family patterns was asking a lot from a course on stressful relationships, but her question led right into the topic for the night.

The previous chapter introduced some advanced disarming movements that we can use to avoid getting stuck when stressed-out people block the road to yes. In this chapter we will present some advanced ways to connect with people and empower them.

Building on What H.E.L.P.S.

Wherever we live, work, or play, there are mine fields of crises and mountains of daily hassles. Everyone we know is exposed to these same explosives and minor irritants. The love we share and the work we do can easily be disrupted. With additional surveillance and support skills, however, we can create homes and workplaces that are more nurturing, productive, and rewarding.

We will continue to use examples from business and professional settings because, as James Autry writes in *Love and Profit*, "Work can provide the opportunity for spiritual and personal, as well as financial growth. If it doesn't, then we're wasting far too much of our lives on it."

Whatever our job, whether we serve drinks or sell homes, treat disease or give manicures, fix cars or teach students, sell groceries or baby-sit, each of us works with people who may be stressed-out. The stress can be either a frustrating barrier or an opportunity to enrich our lives. Knowing how to respond helpfully without overextending ourselves can be of immeasurable importance to each of us.

Advanced support techniques are not any more complex or

complicated than H.E.L.P., they simply allow us to go a little deeper. They are designed to enrich the ongoing personal and occupational relationships in our lives.

Every person's unique experience can be better understood by uncovering ambivalent feelings and discovering the thoughts beneath those feelings. The advanced techniques enrich our relationships because the more we understand, the more effective support we can give and the more true friendship we will share. Did you know that in a study of loving and long-lasting marriages, the most common reason given for marital success was that their partner was their best friend?

Feeling More Than One Way About What's Happening

The emotional turmoil of any stressful situation or crisis usually involves a mixture of intense feelings, both good and bad. This adds to the confusion and upset. Nevertheless when we ask, many people tell us what they think instead of what they feel.

Some people would like to avoid dealing with feelings at all costs. These people either don't trust their feelings or don't want to deal with them because they are too messy. Some hide their anxiety by thinking that it's "wimpy" to talk about feelings. The stronger and wiser person knows that not to deal with feelings is actually the weaker and more foolish path, since ultimately there is a price to pay. Feelings don't go away by being ignored. On the contrary, they get stronger.

It's important to deal with people's resistance to discussing their emotional reactions. Feelings change or resolve by being expressed and acknowledged. When we gently persist in asking people about how the situation affects them, they are more likely to share their emotional responses.

After getting an answer to "How does that make you feel?" probing for additional feelings can often make a big difference in the effectiveness of the support we give. We recommend following up with the question "Any other feelings?" Once mixed feelings are sorted out and accepted, they become less confusing and upsetting.

When people share multiple feelings with us and we accurately reflect back both their emotions and the intensity of those emotions, they feel closer to us. This process can build a special bridge between two people.

The Relationship Between Thoughts and Feelings

The world is full of emotionally neutral occurrences—until we think about them. The meaning we assign to what has happened, is happening, or may happen in our lives determines our emotional responses. Our unique thoughts bring about wide variations in feelings to particular circumstances. This is why so many different things can put people on different angles of tilt.

In crises people often jump to extreme conclusions, take things very personally, and make dangerous caves out of everyday doghouses. When we exaggerate our thinking, we exaggerate our emotional response. To put it simply, people are not disturbed by events but by their interpretations of them.

Many times people may not even be aware of the special significance an event holds for them, and their emotional reactions catch them by surprise. Since we can go on tilt out of joy as well as despair, we recommend asking either, "What thrills you most about that?" or "What troubles you most about that?" and sometimes both. This helps us to tap into their thinking.

H.E.A.L.T.H.Y.

To build on H.E.L.P. and include these powerful questions, we created a new acronym—H.E.A.L.T.H.Y. The A stands for additional or ambivalent feelings ("Any other feelings?"); T for thoughts or themes ("What troubles/thrills you most about this?").

As you can see below, three of the letters (H, E, and L) in

H.E.A.L.T.H.Y. are exactly the same as in H.E.L.P. and Support. In addition two of the steps (the second *H* and the *Y*) are the familiar, last two steps of H.E.L.P. and Support, only reworded. The rewording gives us a memorable new acronym and also offers attractive alternatives to the phrases we've been using in H.E.L.P. and Support. So only the *A* and the *T* in H.E.A.L.T.H.Y. are really new.

People tell us they like the additional power of H.E.A.L.T.H.Y. and find it even more practical than H.E.L.P. because it reminds them of two extra tools for difficult situations.

Steps on the Path to H.E.A.L.T.H.Y.

HAPPENING:	"What's **H**appening in your life?"
EMOTION:	"How are you feeling (emotionally) about that?" / "What **E**ffect is this having on you?"
AMBIVALENCE:	"Any other feelings?"
LISTENING:	"It **L**ooks like you are feeling ____ about ____."
THEME:	"What **T**roubles/**T**hrills you most about that?"
HANDLING:	"How are you **H**andling that?"
YIELDING:	"**Y**es, it seems like you're doing the best you can."

A H.E.A.L.T.H.Y. Interaction

Robin asked Edith to describe exactly how she interacted with her office mate, Johnny, the next week. Here's what she reported.

"As you know, Johnny shares an office with me. Yesterday, late in the afternoon, he slammed in looking totally defeated. It seemed important to ask him what had happened. He said that he was in meetings all day and didn't get any of his regular work done.

"I asked him how that made him feel, and he said, 'Totally frustrated.' I thought about 'H.E.A.L.T.H.Y.' and asked him whether he had any other feelings. He told me that he felt good because his boss had delegated responsibility to him. I reflected back that it looked like he was happy that his boss had confidence in him but that being the company representative cost him time and really put him behind. Then I asked him, 'What about it troubles you the most?' He said that his pile of unanswered phone messages was sky-high and that everyone who called him would see him as irresponsible and incompetent. I was careful not to argue with him as I might have in the past.

" 'How will you handle that?' was my next question. He smiled. 'One phone call and one apology at a time.' 'Yes,' I said, 'that's all you can do. It sounds like a good plan.' His quick smile convinced me that we're finally becoming friends."

"Wow!" Robin was impressed. She added thoughtfully, "I'm going to focus on my relationship with my sister and do that same sort of thing. It must be hard for her always to see me as the competent one. She keeps asking me for advice. Instead of giving it, I'll have to use H.E.L.P. and H.E.A.L.T.H.Y. to support and empower her. There's lots of stuff she does right, but most of the time she's so busy second-guessing herself, she only sees the negative. Then she thinks that she doesn't make good decisions and asks me for advice."

More About "What's *Happening*" in Both Acronyms

H appears in both H.E.L.P. and H.E.A.L.T.H.Y., so let's start by reviewing "What's happening?"

Is your evening ruined when your spouse comes home late and is still in the jaws of something that happened at work? Do you get upset when a co-worker starts crying or explodes with anger, even if it's not at you? Do unreasonable customers infuriate you?

Some people, especially at work, know they are in crisis, but they may fear that they will break down and burst into tears or blow up with anger. To reassure themselves and avoid embarrassment, they may hide their pain and put on a calm, if not happy face. But when we approach them, we can sense the tension in the vibrations surrounding them.

How often have you been struggling with a crisis in your life but somehow made it through the workday without others noticing your preoccupation? Were you ready to absorb new information or make important decisions?

H.E.A.L.T.H.Y. help can be given anytime at home or at work, and especially when we notice anything suggesting that someone is preoccupied. How do we know someone is physically there but not available for our relationship?

We may find them asking questions that we have already answered, looking at their watch, or showing little interest in what we are saying. We need to find out what has happened. Noting their distraction is a good way to start. We can ask, as Edith might have, "You seem preoccupied, Johnny, what's happening in your life?"

Sometimes people don't respond well to this question. What if Johnny had snapped back, "Who asked you? It's none of your business"? If we ask the question in a warm tone of voice with attentive body language, this is very rare. Most of the time it simply means that they are probably so overwhelmed by their crisis that they are withdrawing from people.

If someone does withdraw or snaps back, "It's none of your

business," we may want to say, "I don't mean to pry, but you seemed so upset, and if you need some help, I'm available." Some people will take us up on our offer; others will appreciate that we have respected their privacy. Remember, when faced with a roadblock in communication, breaking through the barrier is not the way to go. Anytime people do not want to talk, back off. Agree and set free.

Less Is More

Time is of the essence when we are at work. Be quick to ask what happened, but be brief. Edith was surprised to learn that listening effectively usually means listening briefly. In most cases encouraging people to go on and on about their situation increases rather than decreases their feelings of helplessness, victimization, and resentment.

Have you ever noticed that when you get upset, the more you describe the details of the insults and injuries you've suffered, the angrier you get? Or perhaps you've noticed that the more you moan, the more depressed you get?

Most people believe more is better, and unfortunately when it doesn't work, they do even more of it.

Moving on to _Emotional_ Effects

Robin admitted that before she took our workshop, she avoided asking people about stress or crises, even when she became aware of their situations. She was sure they'd ask, "Do you have an hour?" and she'd never be able to escape. Robin added that whenever she did ask, the results were exhausting. Certainly that was her experience with her sister. It took too much time and energy to hear the details of all her current (and past) disasters and disappointments.

Robin and Edith are similar and clearly not alone. Think about your own experience. Have you ever finished talking with someone and felt depressed? Chances are the other person was depressed. Ever felt angry? Or assaulted? How about confused or anxious? Usually your reactions mirror those of the person in crisis. As you continue to practice our techniques, you will tune in to your reactions and use that information to help understand and address whatever feelings you encounter.

When people are overwhelmed, they are overwhelming. But by swiftly moving them from the details of their story to their emotional reactions, we can help them label and accept their feelings. When we do this, both of us will feel more competent, and together we can move on to more rewarding activities and experiences.

Listen and Live

Did you know that talking boosts blood pressure and that listening lowers it? At least one respected researcher, James J. Lynch, Ph.D., of the University of Maryland, acknowledges the many contributing factors in high blood pressure but believes that "the condition is most deeply connected to problems in human communication." In one of his studies, involving 178 children and adults, 98 percent had a blood pressure rise whenever they spoke. Thirty hypertensive patients, on medication to lower their blood pressure, also elevated their pressures into the hypertensive range when talking, some even into medically dangerous zones.

Other research at the University of Pennsylvania suggests that it is not passive listening that lowers blood pressure the most. Instead it is calm attention to something or someone outside ourselves. Drs. Aaron Katcher and Alan Beck took people's pressures while they read aloud, stared at a blank wall, and watched fish swimming in a tank. The results? Blood pressure was highest while speaking, but it was lower watching the fish swim than just staring at a wall.

Is there a relationship between stress, attention, and hypertension? It seems that while stress triggers an alarm response that raises blood pressure, calm attention triggers an orienting response that brings blood pressure down. In *The Language of the Heart* Dr. Lynch reports, "We have found that learning to listen to other people can help hypertensives lower their blood pressure ... dramatically—sometimes to lower levels than they had seen in years!"

This is one more reason why we believe that the acronym H.E.A.L.T.H.Y. describes an interaction that enhances everyone's emotional, interpersonal, *and* physical health.

The Second *H* in *H.E.A.L.T.H.Y.*

"How are you handling that?" is the first of the two final steps that are used in both H.E.A.L.T.H.Y. and H.E.L.P.S. There are subtle differences to explore in each rewording.

When we ask, "How are you handling that?" some people will answer how they are handling their feelings and others how they are handling the situation. Both are important pieces of information. When we asked, "What are your plans," in H.E.L.P., people probably gave us how they planned to handle the situation as opposed to how they were handling their feelings. In addition the question about plans generally moves people toward the future and away from old news or feelings. This is usually good, but not always.

Sometimes people answer our question about how they are handling the situation in a very brief or glib way, such as, "Not very well." We can make good use of the subtle difference between *handling* and *planning* by following up this kind of response with "What are your plans?" When we are using H.E.L.P. and get the response "None," we can also make use of the difference by asking, "How are you handling that?"

Asking how people are handling an event allows them to self-assess their coping strategies. In addition it continues to communicate interest in their personal welfare. Furthermore it gives us a chance to assess their decision-making capacities.

On a few occasions when we ask, "How are you handling that?" we will learn that they are engaging in self-defeating or self-destructive behaviors. This is a good thing for us to find out.

At times we may decide to reschedule what we had planned to do. This gives them time to pull themselves together before proceeding. This may be very important in business situations. Later we'll talk about how to handle potentially self-destructive behaviors.

Y Is for _Yes_ and _Yielding_ to the Other Person's Right of Way

Yes is a word people like to hear. _Yes_ is positive. It makes us feel good. _No_ stirs up bad feelings. We want our co-workers, clients, friends, and loved ones to feel good, so it is important to find a way to say yes to them: "Yes, I have a sense of what is happening to you." "Yes, I can understand how this must be a terrible (or thrilling) time for you." "Yes, I think you're reacting as anyone would under these conditions." "Yes, it seems like you're doing the best you can." "Yes, I think you're doing the very best that you can with a tough situation."

By saying yes we are affirming other people. Being affirmed allows them to feel competent and reconnected to their inner resources. They feel healthy.

When people come up with what we think of as hare-brained schemes, it's important to avoid letting feelings of disapproval or criticism creep into our voices. By yielding and keeping our comments positive toward even the weakest of ideas, we are supportive and encourage the person to keep creating options.

In an article describing treatments for addictions, _Newsweek_ quoted actor Tony Curtis's vision of support: "Instead of having bars every few blocks, we should have little therapy centers where you can pull your car over and have a chance to talk to somebody." If more people in more places knew how to listen and yield the right of way, their family, friends, neighbors and co-workers could say where they were going and feel good about how they were traveling. This vision can become an affordable reality. It's up to us.

Keeping Ourselves Off Tilt

Before we go into detail about the new parts of H.E.A.L.T.H.Y., we want to reemphasize the importance of managing our own stress in constructive ways. On tilt we are less able to cope with stressed-out people, and we react automatically with our own fight-flight-or-freeze response. This escalates stress for everyone. Each of us can learn to get support when we need it. We must be sure that when we reach out to others, we have a firm footing. The next four chapters focus on additional ways to H.E.L.P. ourselves before we H.E.L.P. others.

16

Finding Others
When You Go on Tilt

"The greatest gift we can give
is rapt attention to one another's existence."
—AUTHOR UNKNOWN

Steven had just broken up with Corinne, his first serious relationship. As part of a couple for over three years, Steven had drifted away from most of his noncommitted friends. Now, dealing with the pain of his loss, he felt socially isolated. He wasn't sure why the relationship had dissolved and how much of it was his fault. Conflict resolution and communication skills had never been his strengths. Steven was just beginning the difficult process of reconnecting with other people and trying to make sense out of the dramatic changes in his world.

Steven fears that until he gains insight and improves his interpersonal skills, he will only re-create the same stormy and ultimately destructive relationship. In the meantime his loneliness has become a real problem.

Is it more important for Steven to form relationships with more people and enlarge his "support network" or to improve his insight and interpersonal skills?

How about the rest of us? We all find that regardless of how many times we have helped others through any number of life changes, there are rough times when we ourselves feel incompetent and disconnected. How can we get the support we need? Perhaps we need to ask ourselves the same question as Steven. Do we need more or better relationships? While both might be helpful, one is clearly more important.

Quality Versus Quantity

In the late 1980s the surprising answer to this question came from a Yale study of over three thousand people. This research focused on the impact of marital status and interpersonal conflict on depression. As had been expected, single, separated, or divorced people were at much higher risk for depression than were married folk. But another finding was far more significant and totally unexpected.

People who were married but felt unable to share information about important aspects of their lives with their spouses were twenty-five times more likely to become depressed than were those who were able to talk with their spouses. This extraordinary "odds ratio" made it clear that the benefits of marriage were completely reversed when the partners withdrew from each other to avoid conflict.

Other studies showed that when married people are depressed, they have slower recoveries and inferior response to antidepressant medication compared with those who are equally depressed but single. In addition, criticisms from a spouse were a common complaint among the depressed, and they strongly predicted relapse into depression. It is not the legal or social status of being married that is good for our health but the opportunity to share our lives, our hopes, and our burdens with a loving and accepting companion.

For those of us who are single, the support network we build with friends has life-enhancing and lifesaving qualities. Elderly people who can confide in at least one person, whether this is a spouse, friend, or family member, maintain better physical and mental health than those who had no confidant.

Playing the Odds with New Thoughts

So we may need to enlarge our support network but the biggest payoffs may come from improving our interpersonal skills. If our relationships with people were better, we would be able to face crises without becoming as depressed or stressed-out as many of us do. Are we suggesting that we should ignore or dump our current relationships to give ourselves time and energy to search for and forge new ones? No. We recommend a mix of rejuvenating old relationships while being open to finding new ones.

To enhance current relationships, a combination of the four *T*s of trust, time, talk, and touch go a long way toward healing misunderstandings. But to avoid putting all our proverbial eggs into a few current baskets, let's explore ways that we can increase our chances of drawing more supportive people into our lives.

The first two steps in the process are to acknowledge our need for people and to be intentionally open to what occurs. In addition we need to play the odds and apply the law of large numbers. This law says that if a person knocks on enough doors and asks enough people to go out for a cup of coffee or a beer, that person will end up drinking more liquid than any bladder can handle. Unfortunately this law is seldom applied, because the fear of rejection keeps all too many people isolated and lonely.

For most of us, building a strong social support system means finding a few people who accept what we do as the best we can do at this time, who respect our need to grow, and who joyfully encourage us to become everything we can become. The fear of rejection, however, often keeps us in self-destructive relationships and prevents us from finding more fulfilling ones. Let's look at the distorted thinking that creates and maintains this immobilizing fear.

We Experience What We Think About

What are the thoughts that promote fears of rejection? *If I'm feeling this miserable, who'd want to know me? People don't want to be around me when I'm like this. When I meet people, I never know what to say. I'm too fat, skinny, tall, short, hairy, bald, young, old, dumb, intellectual, restless, exhausted, earthy, highbrow, . . .* and the list goes on.

These thoughts are not only exaggerated, they are also self-fulfilling. We not only experience what we think about, we become what we think about. In addition, as the Desiderata instructs, "If you compare yourself with others, you may become vain and bitter; for always there will be greater and lesser persons than yourself."

Changing these thoughts often involves hard work. Before we can change them, we have to become aware of how we habitually limit our interactions based on these erroneous beliefs. It is best to examine our thoughts just before we back away from reaching out.

We need to ask ourselves, *What is my greatest fear about what might happen if I reached out?* These fears are our hidden handicaps. We can benefit by looking at ourselves as though we were nonjudgmental observers and then analyzing the data in a scientific way. It may help to ask, *Is what I'm telling myself completely true? What's the evidence? Where is it written that people with my attributes are not lovable?* and other challenging questions.

By disputing our thoughts we can make room for healthier beliefs and affirmations. Reframing our situations and translating obstacles into welcome and necessary challenges can make a vital difference.

Consider those who have physical handicaps and use wheelchairs. Physical disabilities do not have to prevent people from positive personal interactions. One can project all the wonderful qualities of attractive humanness just as well sitting as standing. Franklin D. Roosevelt led the country from a wheelchair. Recovering from a stroke, one courageous activist helps herself and others who ask about her situation by answering, "I can look at myself as disabled, but I prefer to see everyone else as just 'temporarily abled.'"

Accepting the Risk of Rejection

So, whether our reservations about reaching out to others come from hidden or obvious handicaps, we can choose to overcome them. Sometimes it helps to ask ourselves what the best and worst possible outcomes might be if we take a risk. By looking at the worst-case scenario as though from a distance, we come to realize that the unexamined fears that are holding us back are all bark and no bite. So what if we can't please everybody?

Taking risks, first in imagination and then in real-life situations, can help us realize that we have nothing to fear but the fear of rejection. Unlike the pain from a wound that we can blame on a knife, the pain of rejection comes from believing one has been rejected. As Eleanor Roosevelt said, "No one can make you feel inferior without your consent."

What is the major payoff when we play the odds with new thoughts? When we do things we have been avoiding, our fear decreases and our self-esteem increases. We feel stronger and the world appears to be a safer place.

If We Give the Best We Can, the Best Will Come Back to Us

Once we have met someone, we must give in order to get. By becoming intensely curious about the person we are meeting, we can overcome stranger anxieties and social fears. The gift here is our complete attention to their experience.

The H.E.L.P. format provides a nice structure to guide our initial interaction. It is often best to put our own troubles aside at first so that we can attend to the person we are meeting. Later we can focus on our own events, feelings, and plans.

We can use all the H.E.A.L.T.H.Y. questions early on and we can also ask specific questions about who the other person is, what she likes, and how she chose her occupation, such as "Did you always want to be a ____ ?" Any of these can open the door to shared understandings of the dreams and dramas in our lives. To avoid the trap of occupational roles as identities, we may do well to ask open-ended questions, such as "What do you do for fun?"

Opening Closed Doors

Crises are often the times when we retreat to home, a place where we hope we will always be accepted back, even in the bleakest of times. Being "family" physically, however, is not the same as being close emotionally. This is especially true of the relationship between fathers and sons in our culture. Fathers are often seen as working very hard and sacrificing but not being present for their children. How can we connect when we may need them the most?

Steven wanted to talk with his dad about his problems, but when he tried at New Year's, his father just turned on the football game on the TV. It felt good to do something they'd always done together, but Steven knew he needed more.

By Easter Steven decided that he'd procrastinated long enough. He didn't have a woman in his life and he had very few friends. Steven realized that he'd have to take the initiative if he was going to make any progress in his relationship with his dad. Facing his fears of still another rejection, he put aside his anger over past hurts and asked Steven senior, "Tell me about what it was like for you to have Grandpa as a father."

After some surprise Steven senior talked about his isolation and distance from his dad. As he warmed up to the subject, he mentioned the resentment he had felt and how his self-confidence was undermined by the criticism and lack of support. Steven was taken aback by the similarities in their relationships. When Steven said, "Dad, I feel a lot of the same things, I had a father who was a lot like that," Steven senior's eyes were full of tears. In the months that followed, Steven and Steven senior were able to share as they never had before.

The lesson? By listening to our loneliness, risking rejection, and reaching out to others, especially when we feel needy, we can deepen some of our most important relationships.

Applying What We Know About Boundaries

What about the troubles we want others to support us through? It's best to avoid boring our friends and future friends with the details of what happened. If we want to go into the particulars of our troubles, our enemies would make the most attentive audience. They might be delighted to hear and spread the news.

Remember Joe and Bill from Chapter 6? Even if Joe's co-workers and friends were interested in the details of his drinking and his marriage, talking about these aspects might backfire later. Instead Bill chose to move right on from what's happening to how Joe was feeling about it. He knew that learning the gory details might lead to awkward and embarrassing moments later. If Bill had learned intimate details about Joe's marriage, Joe might feel that he had overexposed himself and would probably have withdrawn farther. We saw this in Chapter 5 when Mr. Jackson backed away from Sally after she learned too much about his personal life.

Bill used H.E.L.P. to avoid crossing important personal boundaries, but most people have not yet learned to respect these limits. Studies show that people who talk about personal issues with a new acquaintance are likely to be seen as "poorly adjusted." Later- or last-born white, middle-class women "spill" more than others in our culture, but we all need to discipline ourselves to keep the boundaries.

We can keep H.E.L.P. in mind here too. When we are tempted to spill everything, we can describe what happened briefly and move right on to our feelings about the event.

If someone asks a none-of-your-business question, we may need to respond with the question that Ann Landers recommends: "Why in the world would you be interested in something so personal?" But most of the time we are the ones who cross the boundaries of intimacy.

Let's Be More Optimistic

Recent research at the University of Pennsylvania suggests that it pays to be optimistic. Optimism yields better overall health, keeps depression at bay, and improves performance. Why? In terms of health, when we think pleasant and hopeful thoughts, our brain cells release different chemicals than when we predict dire consequences. These chemicals travel to all parts of our body and are also natural antidepressants. How does optimism improve performance? Since pessimistic people see failure as general, long-term, and self-generated, they avoid taking the risks that could make them happier and more successful.

These attitudes are self-perpetuating, like the fabled twins, one of whom was an optimist and the other a pessimist. The parents of these twins followed a therapist's advice and on their birthday gave the pessimist a room full of toys and the optimist a box of manure. As we heard the story, the parents then found the pessimist muttering that the toys are only going to break and found the optimist digging through the manure saying, "You can't fool me, where there's manure, there's got to be a pony!"

Our point is simple. Let's be optimistic. Given more than four billion people in the world, it is likely that our efforts will help us connect with some of the people we need. Once we connect, it may help to affirm J.D. Salinger's words: "I am kind of paranoic in reverse. I suspect people of trying to make me happy."

Many Hands Make Helping Easy

Building a network of several supportive relationships is important. One or two loving friends may do more for our self-esteem than dozens of casual acquaintances, but when we need support, if we only have a couple of loving friends, our needs may overwhelm them.

Have you ever tried to lift someone up above your head? Do you think it might be easier if more people were involved? Ever see a victorious team spontaneously carrying the quarterback off the field? To multiply the strength of our mutual support systems, we need ways of finding more hands and working together when we need a lift.

In the next chapter we'll explore some of the best ways to get the help we need from those around us.

17

Asking for Support
and Accepting Help

*"If the knocking at the door is loud and long, it isn't
opportunity—it's relatives."*
                                    —Farmer's Almanac, 1990

Ever wonder why some people get rattled by a telephone
salesperson calling them at home, or why a co-worker writes
the whole day off when the fax needs repair? The more we use
H.E.L.P. in our interactions with stressed-out people, the more
we discover that people have their own, unique set of trigger
points that put them on tilt.

For some it's budget busters, for others car problems, and,
for still others it may be the way we treat them. It can be as
vital as a tight deadline or as trivial as a lost sock. But remember, "vital" and "trivial" are in the eye of the beholder. Ultimately it's the sense of being out of control.

What Kind of Things Put You on Tilt?

Knowing where we are vulnerable gives us more control
over our reactions. If we are aware that last-minute work or-

ders drive us up the wall, we can stay a little ahead, leave some time slots open, or take steps to prevent such orders at their source. When this is not possible, we can prepare ourselves to receive them. In addition, when someone pushes our buttons and puts us on tilt, it doesn't have to ruin our day. We can recover quickly. Recognizing the symptoms makes us feel smart and therefore back in control.

Listing key hassles from memory may be difficult. Keeping a journal, which we discuss in the next chapter, really helps. But whatever it takes to identify what pushes our buttons, the personal knowledge gained is powerful. It may not guarantee us a perfect twenty-four hours of fun, love, and productivity, but it can protect us from overreacting to many annoyances that seemingly wait to pounce on us and disrupt our days.

What's Really the Problem?

When a disruption puts us on tilt, we need to decide which button it is pushing. Is it the "I feel incompetent and defective" button or the "I'm all alone and disconnected" one; the "I feel stupid and don't know enough" one or the "I'm being used and abused" one? A very troubling button for many single people involves the bottom-line issue "My perception and memory of what happened is being challenged."

When what we are doing suddenly stops being fun or challenging and becomes a problem, we need to recognize that we are headed for tilt. At this point it is important to determine what happened and how it is threatening us. The answer to these questions will also tell us which buttons we need to protect or disassemble. For example none of us likes to feel incompetent. So when time lines turn into deadlines that can't be met, this puts us on tilt. Therefore we may need to revise our approach to the task along the way. We may also need to communicate clearly and respond to change by renegotiating the work, the number of workers, or the deadline.

"What Do I Need to Make Me Feel Better?"

Identifying what we need to feel better in a particular situation is essential. We can ask ourselves, "Do I need someone to remind me that I'm competent?" or "Do I need someone to tell me they love me?" "Do I need to find someone to listen to me as I sort out the problem and my options?" or "Do I need to find someone to take on part or all of the problem?"

Are we routinely overloaded and overwhelmed by a constipated lifestyle? If so, we might do well to ask, "Do I need someone to give me permission to let things go, or can I give myself that permission?"

People Want to Know How to Help You

As children our needs were simple and our parents could anticipate most of them. As adults we still have a little person within us who longs for mind-reading caretakers. This leads to much disappointment.

Some of us don't feel that we deserve help unless we are victims of a disaster such as a hurricane or a terrorist bombing. We find it still harder to ask for help when our specific handicaps are "just" raw nerves or hidden scars. Asking for and accepting help may be difficult for us, yet most of us are ready and willing to support other people in our situation. Does that make sense? If not, is it time to change *our* behavior?

"Whom Do I Ask?"

The larger and wider the support network of friends and acquaintances we build, the more resources we can tap when we need help. In single-parent or dual-career families, for example, having a back-up list of child care options is critical. This is particularly true when one suddenly becomes sick.

Making plans in the midst of a crisis is difficult. By anticipating our needs we can get a running start toward fulfilling them. Listing our supporters prior to a crisis gives us a sense of security and preparedness.

Think of your own allies. Who helps you out in a pinch? Who knows you best and loves you anyway? Who listens and doesn't give unrequested advice? Who holds you when you cry? Whom can you count on to make you laugh?

Part of this work also involves listing those friends, neighbors, acquaintances, co-workers, and even family who are not supportive or who might do us a favor but will keep a permanent record of the debt incurred. Others who tend to downplay our pain, rush us through our feelings, or rain on our parade leave us feeling empty and cut off. These people also belong on our not-to-ask list.

We must learn to trust our intuition. If it doesn't feel right, it probably isn't.

"What Specific Help Do I Want?"

Not all hassles are little ones, but regardless of the circumstances or crises, the process of getting support is almost the same. Neil is a management trainee who was just given two-weeks' notice as part of a company-wide "right-sizing."

When the raises and bonuses Neil had been promised didn't materialize, he had respected the realities of the times and had worked still harder. He knew that layoffs were coming, but now that he was faced with the actual event, two questions keep running through his head: "How am I going to pay my bills?" and "How could they do this to me?"

There isn't anyone there to give Neil H.E.L.P., so he gives it to himself. When Neil asks himself how he is feeling, he recognizes that he is scared and angry. By labeling his feelings, he is able to calm down and ask himself specifically what he wants in the way of support.

Neil recognizes that he wants someone to reassure him that he is not incompetent and that he is just one among many who have lost jobs recently. Neil also considers finding allies to bomb the office, but decides it would be better to play some basketball at the YMCA, and get some physical release for all his pent-up anger.

Neil sifts through a list in his mind of people he could ask for reassurance and help. He thinks of Jack, whom he met when he joined the Rotary Club a couple of months ago. Jack had talked about how his firm was laying off a lot of middle managers.

Neil decides to ask Jack to join him at the gym so that he can take out some frustration on the court and get the support he wants. Neil hopes to get both of his needs met with Jack, but Jack's knee has been acting up, so they can only meet for lunch. Neil decides to see if he can find a pickup game at the Y and heads for the gym.

Getting a Little Help from Our Friends

Neil feels better after some hard-driving basketball. He hits the boards as well as ever and even manages a couple of his favorite hook shots. It's a great release, and the shower makes him feel like a new person.

At lunch with Jack the next day Neil feels reassured. As he talks about what happened, he begins to realize how stagnant the job had become. Neil starts to feel some excitement about new opportunities. He makes a point of thanking Jack for listening and reflecting back his ideas.

A few days into the first week after leaving the job, Neil discovers his loneliness. Once again he asks himself the H.E.L.P. questions.

Given his feelings of isolation, Neil decides to join a local job-loss group. He knows that he doesn't want to overload any of his friends by asking too often for too much support, and he hopes the self-help group will make him feel less alone with his problem. Neil wants to get a little help from a lot of friends, but he doesn't want to rely on any one person for total support.

"What Do I Really Need?"

As the days pass, Neil begins more fully to appreciate his situation and to identify more of his feelings and needs. Since his parents are halfway across the country and his last relationship didn't survive his company relocation, aloneness cuts deep. Neil knows that he needs to nurture whatever contacts he's made in the course of networking and begins thinking of the best ways of connecting with each person he's met.

Neil also realizes how much his self-image involves working hard and being productive. Since he's always enjoyed being part of a team, Neil decides to get more involved in the volunteer work through Rotary and church. Not only will it boost his self-esteem and deepen his new friendships but it will help him develop more skills and demonstrate his competence to other volunteers, many of whom are from the business community.

How to Avoid Unwanted Advice

Like Neil, most of us can identify a few people who listen but don't try to fix our problems, give us unwanted advice, or tell us their war stories. Most of us also know not to ask for the suggestions or experiences of others unless we want to hear them.

If we stay on tilt for more than a few days, people near us may get anxious. They are concerned for us and concerned that they will have to adapt to our change and its effects on their life for a long time. This is when an attack of advice often comes, especially from men, who tend to want to fix things and bolster their sense of competence. This is also when an attack of "let me tell you my terrible story so you'll stop feeling so depressed" often comes, especially from women, who tend to want to connect but may do just the opposite. We use the word *attack* because one of the best responses is a form of disarming aikido.

The attack may make us feel incompetent, disconnected, or both, but accusing the person of generating these feelings usually only escalates their advice giving—"Oh, don't be so sensitive"—or alienates us still further.

Rather than starting a fight or ignoring the advice, we can acknowledge or pretend that they are trying to be supportive. If we are concerned that they may expect us to follow their advise, we can make it clear that we are collecting suggestions from all over. We can also clarify our need to solve our own problem or to be given time to see if our solutions pay off.

We can respond to an attack of advice by belly breathing and calmly saying, "I know you're trying to be helpful, but right now I'm just trying to sort through my feelings and figure out what I need." Most advisers will respect our requests to back off when we state them directly. If not, we can repeat the request using slightly different words, so that it acts like a broken record but doesn't sound like one.

The Importance of Being Clear

Maggie is a friend of ours who works as a civil servant. Months after a new secretary was assigned to Maggie, the secretary continued to make a lot of mistakes, especially when pressed for time. When she was not on tilt, she demonstrated superior secretarial skills. The biggest problem, however, was how the secretary handled herself after she made a mistake. She would accuse Maggie of giving vague and confusing directions and of never being satisfied. Almost every week the secretary's administrative supervisor would ask Maggie to explain why she was hassling the secretary.

This problem took up countless hours of their time, and the increased stress took its toll on the quality of Maggie's work and her personal satisfaction. The solution? Maggie explained to the secretary what to do when she pointed out a mistake. Specifically our friend asked the secretary to say, "I'm sorry it happened, what would you like me to do now?"

Once Maggie clarified what she wanted and asked for it firmly, the problem vanished, never to be seen again. A fairy tale? No. The results could be predicted because, as co-creators of all our relationships, other people tend to interact with us the way we teach them to interact with us.

Asking for Feedback

The idea of checking with others about their willingness and ability to help may seem obvious, but it is often overlooked. Too often we assume that because we've helped people or they've helped us in the past, they can and will help us now. By asking we increase the odds of getting support, while we decrease the odds of disappointment and alienation.

We can also ask others for feedback about how they see us handling things. In a crisis we tend to move too fast or act too slowly, and we can often use an objective opinion about our timing. If we want to encourage our friends to give us level-one feedback about our behavior, we might just ask, "What do you see me doing?" If we are concerned about their response to our changes, we might also request level-two feedback. Finally, it may be helpful to get their opinion about the possible consequences of our behavior in the form of level-three feedback. More about this in Chapter 22.

When Others Say, "No, I Won't Help."

Occasionally someone may turn down our request for help. Perhaps they feel burdened or on tilt themselves. Their angry response to our request, or ours to their refusal, can teach us to toughen our skin and sharpen our interpersonal skills. Are we coming across as too needy? Angry responses can prompt us to look at how we ask for support and what pushes our anger button when our needs are not met.

Maybe we don't feel anger in these situations. Do we feel hurt, shame, guilt, or anxiety? Specifically, how do we feel when we ask for what we want and yet fail to get it or receive less than what we wanted? Do we feel inadequate as human beings? Unloved or unlovable? These questions can start us on a journey of insights about our lives. We may not enjoy the experience, but we can be certain that if we're ready to learn, it can teach us something.

Keeping Expectations Realistic

By disarming ourselves and our helpers we can avoid overreacting, remain calm, and stay positive. Once we have requested a favor or support, it may be best to lower our expectations. When we are content with less, we have more.

To get help, we need to practice making the right requests of the right person at the right time. This pays off for everyone involved.

"Yes, But . . ."

Some of us get help from our social network but still continue to complain. Research suggests that people who complain, despite the attempt of others to be helpful, lose the support they generate.

One of the most important patterns to avoid is called "Yes, but." A friend who makes a series of well-meaning reflections or suggestions only to hear "Yes, but that's not really how I feel," "Yes, but that wouldn't work," or "Yes, but I couldn't do that" will eventually withdraw from these unpleasant experiences.

If we try to delegate or share tasks but can't really let go, we can get into another brand of "Yes, but . . ." that drives help away. When someone sees that we are overloaded, for example, and asks, "What can I do?" we must decide if the person is trustworthy and if we want to trust him or her to take over some part of our responsibility. If not, we need to say no politely but firmly. Otherwise the message "Yes, I want you to do this, but I don't trust you" will undermine not only our friend's support, but the relationship itself.

Giving Helpers Feedback

Instead of "Yes, butting," we need to give supporters balanced feedback on how they are helping us. This is particularly true in situations where men have listened supportively and have expressed their reactions without trying to fix the problem. It is equally important in those situations where women might offer support in the form of practical assistance without talking about their own experiences. In order to bring out the best in people, we need to ask for it and acknowledge it. Clearly we get what we teach people to give.

We also need to redirect the efforts of helpers when what they do is not helpful. We can thank them and point out, in nondemanding ways, what we would experience as more helpful in these situations.

Finally, we need to show our gratitude in word and deed. There are commercial cards and gifts, but one of the most touching might be a handwritten note that reads, "You were really there for me. It made all the difference. Thank you for being part of my life."

Just because this advice sounds simple and obvious doesn't mean that it's unimportant or easily followed. We often hold fast to the common belief that genuine support should be spontaneous, need no guidance, and require no expression of appreciation.

When we seek family support, we are often the most disappointed. Many of us hold on to unrealistic expectations that family members will know what we want, respond to our needs, and continue meeting them without specific requests, directions, or gratitude. In addition, in established relationships we tend to depend on old patterns that may be ineffective in the new, crisis situation.

In the next chapter we offer ways to give ourselves support and foster our own growth by exploring the many benefits of keeping a journal.

18

Journaling:
Self-Support Revisited

"Pain is inevitable, but misery is optional."
—Quoted by CHRISTINA BALDWIN at her journal workshop

To call it an upsetting day would be an understatement, Ellen thought. Murphy's Law was the only thing that operated flawlessly. Everything that could possibly go wrong went wrong. Computers were down for several hours and the phones never stopped ringing. Customers who had been put on hold for too long became infuriated when they were told that no appointments could be scheduled because of malfunctioning equipment. An executive had a screaming fit like a three-year-old when he learned that an important caller couldn't get through the busy lines. By the end of the day Ellen felt as though she had spent eight hours in a combat zone.

She felt tired, hungry, and cranky and did not look forward to the meeting she planned to attend that evening. Ellen knew that unless she shook this mood, she would only lose friends and alienate people.

Arriving at her small apartment, Ellen breathed a sigh of relief. She didn't have to talk to anybody. There were some real advantages to living alone. Ellen heated some soup and opened her journal to a blank page. She wrote H.E.L.P.

Journaling

Whether we wish to supplement our social support or begin a joyous journey inward, a journal is a wonderful way to wash off the day's grime, recharge our batteries, and jump-start personal growth. The personal journal provides a way to reflect on our experience and center ourselves when we are on tilt. It also provides a vehicle for retaining the important details of our lives so that we can tap their richness. When we reach out and experience the pain of rejection, journaling an account of it helps to identify and acknowledge the hurt and to make sense of it. Using H.E.L.P. and H.E.A.L.T.H.Y. as a structure when we are upset or otherwise emotionally aroused facilitates the process and enables us to be self-supporting.

Sipping her soup, Ellen looked at the acronym H.E.L.P. and considered what was happening. She wrote, "Rotten day at work. Computers down. Tempers up. Everyone screaming. I really tried to be supportive. I ducked. I tried to disarm people. I agreed that the system was absurd and that we should have a backup. I didn't blame people for getting upset. But the complaints just kept coming, and no one acknowledged what a good job I was doing."

Then she thought about what emotion she felt. "Unappreciated," she noted.

The L which stands for Listening in H.E.L.P., can be used by the journal writer as a way to reflect on the experience. Ellen wrote, "Looks like I handled things quite well, under the circumstances. I kept my cool, I was aware of applying those disarming techniques that I had learned in the stress class. And they worked. Mr. Grayson was very angry when he missed his call. He really lost control. I guess it must have been important. Knowing him, tomorrow he will probably apologize all over the place. But right at the moment I feel very unsupported."

Looking at the *P*, Ellen thought about her plans. "Tonight I'm going to my meeting and I'm going to think about things other than work. There are a couple of very interesting people in the group that I would really like to get to know better. I also have to think about going back to school. Being a telephone operator is a good learning experience, but I really want to do something where I can have a greater impact on people's lives."

Ellen smiled. She felt much better. She had given herself very effective support and was now ready to relate to other people.

When she sat down to write in her journal, Ellen had been very clear about what was bothering her. H.E.L.P. was useful in quickly coming to grips with the situation. At other times, when she had been more confused or the situation had been more complex, she would write her responses to H.E.A.L.T.H.Y.

Journaling H.E.A.L.T.H.Y.

After recording the day's events (*H*) and her emotional reaction (*E*), she would go on to the other letters in H.E.A.L.T.H.Y. and write about *A*—any other feelings. Somehow, having a pen in hand allowed the flood of feelings to pour out onto the paper. Often she was surprised by the intensity of her reactions, and she was relieved once they were recorded. Her reflections (*L*) allowed her to see when she was overreacting. Then she would use the *T* to think about what old themes and personal meanings might have resonated with the events and triggered her strong reactions. The second *H* would prompt her to question how she was handling the situation and to plan to make necessary changes. She would finish by using *Y*—to say yes and to acknowledge that she was doing a terrific job. After all, she was becoming self-aware, being introspective without obsessing, and using her insights to enable her to reach out to other people.

Beyond First Aid

The *T* in H.E.A.L.T.H.Y. gets at our thoughts behind those situations that cause us to overreact. We can use the pages of a journal to ask, "Why am I reacting so strongly to this? Is there someone or something that this reminds me of?"

If our requests of others are consistently denied, for example, it may be helpful to review our journal to reconsider both the people we ask and the ways we ask. Are we asking the wrong people for too much, too vaguely?

We don't get to choose our parents or our childhoods. If our relationship with our parents was flawed by an early loss or we grew up in a dysfunctional family lacking emotional nourishment, we may develop extreme fears about separation and reenact self-defeating relationships that are too close or too distant. By journaling we may review the early traumas and discover, for example, that we need to change, leave, or let go of certain relationships that reinflame or mirror the past. In this way we can make room for more fulfilling relationships in the future.

Journaling is a great denial buster. Sometimes we need to face what we've lost and cry about it before we can accept and grow from the loss.

Maybe Ellen had been writing about how she felt after dropping out of college when her father died in order to help support the family. For a long time she had felt stuck, as many of us do when we feel helpless and hopeless. She was sure that she had lost the opportunity for an education, possibly forever. One approach we can use in these situations is to respond in our journal to the following series of three questions:

1. What do I feel?
2. What do I want?
3. What can I do about it?

Sometimes Ellen filled a page with "If only's" before asking herself what she was feeling. If only her father hadn't died. If only there was more money. When she asked herself, *What do I feel?* she realized how sad, lonely, and guilty she felt. The more she wrote, the more she got in touch with her resentment. She wrote in her journal about the guilt she felt for blaming her mother and about the basic unfairness of life. It was the inability to let go of the resentment that made her feel stuck. When she asked herself, *What do I want?* she recognized that she wanted to go back to school. *What can I do about it?* helped her to make plans for taking courses and ultimately obtaining a degree in a field that would allow her to work constructively with people.

By labeling her feelings Ellen finds them less intimidating and is then able to ask herself specifically what she wants and what she can do about it.

A journal is a wonderful place for self-discovery. It's as if we are tapping an inner therapist. The only cost is an investment of our time and attention.

Understanding Relationships Through Journaling

Steven writes how when he was eight, Steven senior was shipped out to fight halfway around the world. Steven wished his father had taken more time to say good-bye with more feeling and had written him his own letter and described how much he missed playing catch and fishing.

Steven then asks himself what he can do to gain understanding about his significant relationships, first with his exgirlfriend, Corinne, and then with his father. He writes down different ways that he could express these thoughts and feelings to Corinne and Steven senior. Steven then drafts two honest and moving letters in his journal, one to his former lover and the other to his father.

In his letter to Corinne, for example, he traces the history of their relationship, his frustration and his pain. He is able to see for the first time that his unrealistic expectations had made it impossible for her to please him. Her urgency to set a date for their wedding had frightened him. His own tendency to keep his feelings to himself and to avoid addressing conflicts clearly prevented the resolution of their differences.

Working in his journal makes Steven feel that he will be able to communicate more effectively in his next relationship. He has no need to send the letter. The clarity he achieves by writing it in his journal is a gift that he gives to himself. He uses the letter to his father as the basis of a telephone call to expand on their Easter discussion and to reaffirm their improved relationship.

Journaling as a Lifestyle

Even those of us who have survived serious childhood traumas can benefit from journaling about the experience. When we are growing up, our emotions develop before our reasoning abilities. As adults we can affirm and reassure our inner children by putting words to what happened, what we felt, and how it affected our lives. An excellent resource for men and women survivors of childhood sexual abuse who wish to journal about their experience, for example, is The Courage to Heal Workbook by Laura Davis.

Studies have shown increased self-esteem following just a few weeks of writing about personal traumas. In one study, mentioned earlier, the group of college students who journaled not only felt better but earned higher grades the following semester than a control group of students who did not put their thoughts on paper. Another study documented that college freshmen who wrote about experiences that were disturbing made fewer visits to the college health service during the academic year than freshmen whose writing assignments were less emotionally releasing. Blocking our emotions has physical consequences. Writing in a journal allows us to let go of negative feelings that obstruct our path to health.

Keeping a journal is nothing new. Historically Socrates may have begun the discipline. Famous diarists abound. Emily Dickinson wrote, "I don't know what I think until I read what I say."

Some writers use multicolored pens to journal home, work, love, and friendship, for example. In this way they can review one relationship or area of their life more quickly. Journals can be used to record memories of our past and plan our course for the future. A journal is an opportunity to carry on a dialogue with ourselves.

Journals can also be used to log experiments, record racing speeds, and monitor habits such as smoking, eating, and exercise. The very act of logging an unhealthy behavior brings it to awareness. We can use logs introspectively to note emotions that may trigger the habit and that need our attention in more direct ways. In addition studies show that just monitoring the behavior tends to temporarily decrease its frequency.

Journaling About Changes at Work and at Home

If we've recently left or lost a job, we may recognize how stagnant the job had become and feel some relief as well as some excitement about new opportunities. Using H.E.L.P. and H.E.A.L.T.H.Y. as a springboard to write about our experience in a journal, we may also discover our loneliness. Once we know our feelings, our needs, and our motives, we can plan ways to develop both new job skills and new friendships. Self-employment can be equally isolating. Many customers, suppliers, and others are also self-employed or searching for a job and can become sources of social support. We can explore these options in our journal.

Whatever happens at work can be grist for the mill of our

writing. We spend nearly a third of our lives at work. It can be an important place for personal as well as occupational growth. Keeping a journal can help us realize our potential for success in both.

C-Solutions

When we face problems at work or at home, it helps to search for creative solutions. To open up options, we can search for C-solutions. The letter C can remind us that even when A or B are unattractive, there are always more options. Much of the time, when we are accurately able to sort out our feelings and desires, the character of the problem changes, and solutions that had previously eluded us present themselves.

Life and death are the only absolutes in life, but even here both scientific and spiritual explorations are suggesting there may not be any either-or choices. Medicine struggles with people who are brain dead but alive, and even psychiatrists write about the analysis of past lives.

"Life Is a Daring Adventure or Nothing at All" —Helen Keller

One of the authors found that by wondering what he was going to write in his journal later helped him to become more open to the day's adventures. Suffering with a bad back, he opted to use a wheelchair at the medical center so that he could still lead one of his favorite seminars for medical students about the family in Family Medicine. He'd never been in a wheelchair.

That night he wrote, " 'Handicap-accessible' has a totally new meaning now. Yesterday it was a long, funny-looking and seemingly never-used ramp or a little larger bathroom stall with cold steel bars or a parking space that I would belatedly realize wasn't miraculously reserved for me. Today I almost fell backward going over 'speed bumps' in the form of doorjams.

When I got stuck in a handicap-accessible bathroom, I learned how long and helpless it feels to wait for someone to rescue me. I learned to ask for help after hoping someone would offer it. It was a long, hard day, but help came in unexpected ways from unexpected people.

"I came away aware of how much people enjoyed helping me and how foolish and prideful I'd been to avoid asking for their help in the past. I also found tears in my eyes, not so much from the back pain but from the realization that the cold and impersonal place I'd entered five years before had become a second family of sorts. Yes, we have our family squabbles, but there is a wonderful sense of community when someone is hurting."

Experience is a masterful teacher in so many areas of our lives. What we write about does not have to be dramatic or unusual. In fact Annette Covatta, a Catholic nun and teacher of journaling for personal transformation, says, "Out of the familiar, the life you know, comes the potential for new life." Others call it soul jogging to create meaning.

Revelry

Journaling is one way to avoid sleeping through life. Too often we use drugs, alcohol, or food to dull our heads, our hopes, and our hearts. Rushing forever forward toward unfocused and media-created goals can rob us of all the spaciousness and specialness of time. If we are not mindful of the exciting newness, adventure-filled moments, and pure abundance of daily life, we will endure a boring existence rutted by old patterns, covered with hollow habits, and rattling with rusty chains of sameness.

Journals can wake us up to the richness of everyday experience. While a diary can alert us to danger, the tendency to focus on our troubles can be circumvented by banishing the goblins of fear, savoring the moment, and letting the sun shine in. Our world is bursting with meaning if we use our imagination to understand and describe what life has taught us each day.

Speaking of imagination, journals can also be used to record dreams. Many of us are not in touch with the wealth of insight and unconscious power that is released when we pay attention to the fascinating material of our dreams. By writing down our dreams we preserve a potential treasure that can be mined at any time to shed additional light on the meaning of our day-time experiences. There is a sense of wonder and harmony that develops when we give ourselves the gift of paying serious attention to both our inner and our outer lives.

A journal can help us live our life as a piece of art—a microcosm of the human experience. Keeping a journal furthers the discovery of our unique gifts and joys. We can generate some wonderful feelings of self-acceptance when we place enough importance on our experience to write about it. This kind of self-acceptance is the essence of self-support.

Cramp-Free Writing

If we have problems getting started or getting closure journaling, we may need to avoid perfectionistic goals and replace them with more realistic and desirable goals. We can start with a few lines each day. That's what makes H.E.L.P. so effective. For some of us writing at the same time and in the same place is best. For others it's carrying three-by-five-inch cards and using them to journal while waiting for anything, anywhere. For still others storing the journal in a locked cabinet reassures them that no one else on the planet need ever read their markings.

It is generally useful to start with H.E.L.P. and H.E.A.L.T.H.Y., but there are other questions that are useful in helping us to sort out our reactions to our life experience. One exercise prescribed by Christina Baldwin suggests writing down twenty-five questions that expand the questions "What am I really thinking about?" or "How do I want to spend my life?" As Rainer Maria Rilke wrote on April 23, 1903, in *Letters to a Young Poet,*

> "Be patient toward all that is unsolved in your heart and try to love the *questions themselves.* . . . Do not now seek the answers, which cannot be given you because you would not be able to live them."

Adding the word *and* . . . or . . . *but* at the end of a sentence can help explore deeper feelings or uncover ambivalent ones. It helps to remember that we are not writing to be read but rather to get intimately in touch with our own story. If at some later date we want to summarize things in an autobiography, we can shape it up for reading by spouse, family, friends, or even beyond.

Keeping the document private also frees us up. It allows us to record what might seem to others to be unacceptable or irrational reactions to life's circumstances. There is some evidence, in fact, that people who keep journals meant for posterity do not always record the truth. Since scrupulous honesty is essential if we are to gain accurate self-understanding and self-acceptance, our recommendation is to see the journal as meant for "writer's eyes only."

Renewal

Most of all, the experience of writing should be rewarding and joyful. For many of us a journal can help us remember that it's never too late to develop a childlike curiosity and wonder about the world. Humor is especially welcome. Maybe Zsa Zsa Gabor was journaling when she came up with her comment about her divorces: "I am a marvelous housekeeper. Every time I leave a man, I keep his house." After all, if we don't laugh at ourselves, there'll be plenty of volunteers who'll do it for us.

In many ways the next chapter, which is about getting started helping others, also applies to getting started with the self-support we've discussed in this section.

19

You Can't Learn to Swim
If You Don't
Go in the Water

Do it and learn it,
or regret it.

The only way to learn a skill is to do it. And there are only a few requirements we need to meet before we can start doing it.

First we need to know what the skill will do for us. Then we need to see the skill demonstrated. After the demonstration it's important to break the process down into smaller parts so that they can be learned one at a time. We've done this. Now it's time to put everything we've learned into practice.

Role-play to Learn the Strokes

In our workshops we don't ask people to sit through a lecture about listening. Instead after a brief introduction everyone finds a partner to rehearse and role-play the aikido disarming techniques. Then people practice the H.E.L.P. and

H.E.A.L.T.H.Y. ways of exploring their stress and providing support for each other.

After each encounter the person disarmed or supported gives feedback to the one trying out the new skill. This feedback is even better than a video replay because the recipient of the coping skill can offer not only what was observed but the feelings that the encounter generated.

We invite everyone to process his or her own unique reactions to the experience. How did it feel to ask the H.E.L.P. questions? Was there an impulse to solve the problem or to share a similar experience, rather than fully listening and affirming the other person? How did it feel to receive help when someone used H.E.A.L.T.H.Y. to understand our stress and support us?

Rehearsing and role-playing are a little like the land drills most of us practiced when we were learning swim strokes before we tried them in the shallow end of the pool. If you have an interested friend, you can role-play without a workshop.

Many of us also agree to use H.E.L.P. or H.E.A.L.T.H.Y. routinely whenever we meet. The opportunity to practice the skill repeatedly with someone safe helps to make it automatic and natural.

Don't Start in the Deep End

One of the best places to start learning to swim is the shallow end of the pool. It helps to start using our new communication skills with friends who are experiencing routine stresses. They may be on tilt, but they should not be in deep water.

The first few situations should be confidence-building ones that we could normally have handled without our new skills. This gives us a chance to enjoy the benefits in low-risk encounters. In addition, since most of us are more anxious in an outright attack or an angry retreat situation, it is often easier and more fruitful to start by giving H.E.L.P. and Support to people who are hurting than by disarming people who are angry.

It's a little like job or college interviews. By arranging the least important or least stressful ones first, we can warm up a little and get some practice before we face the big ones.

Getting Our Feet Wet

Before using our new skills with some of the more stressed-out people we know, it helps to practice in our mind's eye. Mental rehearsal not only helps us to perfect our skills, it will also take some of the rough edges off and build our confidence. In addition, if we focus on communicating rather than on performing, we will be free to connect rather than to compete.

It also helps to remember here what we've said before, that anything worth doing is worth doing awkwardly at first. By keeping our sense of humor and lowering our expectations, we will be more open to learning and using new skills.

Let's Not Get in Over Our Heads

While we are learning and building our skills and staying close to the edge, we need to choose carefully to keep from drowning. We should try the techniques with people who are annoyed rather than enraged, for example, and with those who are frustrated following a minor inconvenience rather than with those who are devastated by a major life crisis. After a while we will feel safe going out a little farther.

The Buddy System

Disarming or supporting others can be difficult unless we can discuss with someone how it went. Feedback helps us reach our goals. Stressed-out people are too overwhelmed to give us balanced feedback, and stressed-out situations may be too overwhelming for us to learn from them.

Going it alone is a little like swimming alone. It's just not as much fun, and sometimes it can be risky. Unlike swimming solo, practicing these skills without feedback is not dangerous, but doing so can be less rewarding. We may expose ourselves unnecessarily to embarrassment, discomfort, or misunderstanding. Having a friend to help us sort out the consequences is very helpful.

The buddy system works here much as it does in swimming. It's always important to keep track of our buddy's whereabouts. By teaming up with someone who is interested in practicing these skills and in working with us to get and give feedback, we can accelerate each other's learning. In addition, if we get discouraged, our buddy is there to give us H.E.L.P. and Support.

Swimming Takes Practice

Like swimming, coping with stressed-out people takes practice. It is said that repetition is the mother of skill, and nowhere is that more true than in communication skills. As long as we get good feedback to be sure that we are repeating the right strokes, the more we use these skills, the more automatic, natural, and effective they become.

We can also learn to self-monitor. Raising our awareness to observe our own and other people's body language will provide important information and enhance our skills. What kinds of reactions do we get as we interact with people? What works best? What is the most difficult part? This mindful practice will help us to become more perceptive and improve our communications.

We can practice wherever there are people. It will enhance our sense of personal competence as we connect more constructively with them.

Yes, there are obstacles to practicing, including fear, self-doubt, and feeling overwhelmed by the extent of another person's problems. To motivate ourselves, we may need to redefine our goals in ways that are more meaningful to us. Disarming and reaching out can be seen as part of larger goals, such as bringing harmony to our community or contributing in small ways to world peace.

On a day-to-day level, however, our goal may only be to have one positive interaction with one other person. There is great satisfaction in seeing a stressed-out person relax and smile, even temporarily, in the midst of a crisis. It feels so much better than enduring their attack, withdrawal, or emotional distance.

Overcoming Fear

Sensing even the smallest risk, many of us back away from opportunities to use the skills we are learning. As Shakespeare wrote, "Our doubts are traitors and make us lose the good we oft might win by fearing to attempt."

Fear of the water keeps a lot of people from learning how to swim. A skilled instructor will encourage learners to slowly get used to the feeling of floating while being supported. Learning to put one's face in the water comes next. Controlling our breathing is a big part of learning to swim, as it is in managing stress. It really is a question of feeling in control.

The fear of failure can be addressed by questioning the meaning of the word *failure*. In reality there are no failures. There are only outcomes. Sometimes we are not happy with those outcomes initially, but there is always something to be gained. Legend has it that Thomas Edison said he never had any failures, only learning experiences. Another way of looking at poor outcomes is to label them as "incompletes" rather than failures.

Inviting Others into the Pool

In an earlier chapter we discussed ways to widen and deepen our social network. As we put those principles to work, we may need to give ourselves permission to spend time with people. Keeping our doors open at work, for example, can send an important message about our openness and availability. Unless we respond warmly and openly when people come in, however, we will give them double messages and ultimately disconnect ourselves.

Knowing and respecting our comfort zones for both confrontation and intimacy is also important. Stretching these zones may be necessary; overextending them may be self-defeating.

We may even recommend this book or loan it to people in our social network. This is a good way to find a helping buddy.

Testing Our Buoyancy

Most of us doubt ourselves when we try new things until we enjoy success or lower our expectations about what we "should" be able to do at a given stage of learning. Sometimes it helps to list our communication assets, such as interest in other people, ability to listen, and perseverance. Keeping these in mind helps to lift self-doubt.

In addition we need to acknowledge our successes. We can do this best by recognizing "small wins." Rather than expecting ourselves to be able to disarm a bulldozing boss or to comfort a terrified parent, for example, we need to give ourselves credit for simply recognizing when our old patterns of counterattacking or helping are not working. Maybe we can give ourselves a point for knowing that we could have done better, two points for thinking of what we should have said soon after a difficult encounter, three points for using part of a technique, and so on.

When we slip back into old habits, we don't have to berate

ourselves. This outcome simply suggests that we need to continue to practice the strokes. They have not yet become automatic. Learning and persistence are the keys to achieving our goals. We need to quiet our inner critic, acknowledge our progress, and stay in our lane.

Once We Learn to Swim, We Can Enjoy the Water

Fortunately our brain is a pattern-making system, and over time, our methods of disarming and supporting become as natural and automatic as reading and writing. The fun part of these coping skills is that each encounter is like a chapter in a story or a journal. Each one is new and different. At first all this change and richness of experience may be anxiety-provoking. After a while we look forward to the variety and the creativity in the interactions.

Now it is time to dive in. Once in a while we may get a little water up our nose, but the discomfort is temporary. In addition, if we try to give too much to too many people who are too disturbed, the anxiety may overwhelm us and our excitement could turn to exhaustion. This is a sign that it may be time to climb out and rest.

In the next section we will explore ways to add depth to our helping relationships. The focus will be on the thoughts and feelings that emerge when we find ourselves in life's most dangerous and challenging currents.

PART IV

BUILDING
H.E.A.L.T.H.Y.
RELATIONSHIPS

20

Uncovering Ambivalence

*Ambivalence is both wanting it all
and wanting to get away from it all.*

Like the comic strip "Good News, Bad News," most of what happens to us is a mixture of good and bad. Things that thrill us may also trouble us. Losing a job that we hate may bring both fear and excitement.

We Can't Expect Them to Know What They Feel

Stressed-out people vary in their ability to get in touch with their feelings. For some, the feelings gush out; for others, they get dammed up.

When we ask, "How does that make you feel?" and people say, "I feel that it's not fair," or "I feel that he's trying to hurt me," they are not telling us what they feel, they are telling us what they think. When someone uses the word *feel* followed by some "facts" or an opinion, it does not qualify as a genuine feeling. Anytime someone starts with "I feel *that* . . . ," don't be fooled, it's not a feeling. We'll know it's a feeling when they name emotions, such as "I feel angry" or "I feel scared."

We can usually help people get in touch with their feelings by repeating or rephrasing the E question in H.E.L.P. A couple of good alternatives are "How are you reacting to that?" and "What's that like for you?"

Some people talk about feelings to avoid feeling them. By asking, "What are you feeling now?" we can help them feel current feelings rather than talk about old ones. When people start by saying, "I feel that . . . ," they are focusing on thoughts rather than on feelings.

When we ask the A question in H.E.A.L.T.H.Y.—"Do you have any other feelings?"—the person may shift easily from thoughts or old feelings to present feelings. If we succeed, we can gently invite him or her to get in touch with still more feelings by asking, "Are you feeling anything else?"

There is another advantage to the A in H.E.A.L.T.H.Y. Sometimes a person's feelings are gushing out. They may be enraged, overjoyed, depressed, or frightened. If we use E and ask them how they are feeling, they may wonder if we are paying attention. A few may snap back, "How do you think I'm feeling?" We can answer, "I just wanted to make sure that I knew what you were feeling." With the A question we can also respond, "I just wondered if you had any other feelings about . . ." and thus help them get in touch with additional feelings.

Some Bad News and Some Good News About Feelings

Why is it so important to get to feelings and explore ambivalent ones, especially when we are reaching out to a loved one on tilt? Let's look at some of the worst consequences of avoiding feelings. We do so not to scare anyone but to motivate us all to listen to those closest to us.

Unrecognized and suppressed anger, for example, not only slowly undermines marriages and families, but studies show that it can kill. Men who keep anger bottled up inside are twice as likely to die of heart disease as those who express it. In a marriage where both partners hold anger in, the wife is four times as likely to die of heart disease as wives in marriages where at least one spouse lets it out. In addition people who fail to find healthy expressions for their feelings often substitute excess food, alcohol, drugs, work, TV, or sex.

Fortunately we are learning ways to help the people we love to express their feelings. We encourage using H.E.A.L.T.H.Y. ways to communicate before emotions heat up, smolder, or boil over. As soon as we recognize and validate feelings, they can become more manageable.

Up Is Down and In Is Out

On the roller coaster of life when we're up, we may feel down, and when we're in, we may feel left out. When a couple has a baby, for example, most people think it should be the happiest time of their lives. Starting a family is wonderful, but it is also stressful.

Consider marital satisfaction. Studies show that it plunges after the first baby's arrival and creeps back up only as the children grow up. Babies smile and coo for us. They also cry and wake us up. One wise grandfather described the ambivalence of early parenthood this way: "One minute babies are so cute, you could eat them up . . . and the next minute you wished you had!"

Let's say the couple has a second baby. The first child, who was in, feels out, regardless of how well the parents prepared that child for the birth. The excitement over a new playmate is offset by other big changes, such as having to share the parents' attention. Maybe it's not surprising that some children ask their mother when she's going to bring the baby back to the hospital. Babies are not the only gifts we sometimes feel like returning.

Good Luck Brings Mixed Emotions

Bruce comes home from the factory, sweeps his wife, Marie, into his arms and announces, "I got the promotion, a five-grand raise and I'm a supervisor!" Bruce and Marie get dressed in their best and celebrate at their favorite restaurant. Things couldn't be better.

Three weeks later Bruce is slumped in his new recliner. He has come home early, but he doesn't seem to know what to do with himself. Marie is confused and a little worried. Usually she would ask him why he's moping and get a quick, defensive "I'm not." Marie decides instead to use the H.E.A.L.T.H.Y. way that she learned at church.

Marie sits in the chair next to Bruce and in an uncritical but concerned voice she slowly asks, "Bruce, what's happening?"

"Oh, I don't know, I guess it was a busy day," Bruce offers cautiously.

Marie asks, "How do you feel about that?"

Bruce answers hesitantly, "I guess it's good. I'm proud I'm a supervisor and I'm not worrying as much about our bills."

Marie waits, searches his eyes, and asks, "Any other feelings?"

"Well, yeah, it's a little funny being the boss. It's kinda lonely, I guess."

"It looks like you're feeling both good and bad about the new job," Marie reflects. When Bruce nods, Marie asks, "What troubles you most about it?"

Bruce thinks for a moment and answers, "Well, I don't know, I guess I miss the joking and going places with the guys after work."

Since Marie had noticed the change in Bruce over the last few days, she felt that she knew how he was handling it. So she asked, "What are your plans?" Bruce looked puzzled and asked, "What do you mean by plans?"

Marie wasn't sure what to say, but remembered the importance of focusing on strengths and repeating questions that aren't answered, so she responded, "Well, you're usually pretty good at figuring out how to improve things, so I wondered if you'd thought about it?"

Bruce looked at her and said, "No, I knew this supervisor's job'd be extra responsibility. I expected that. And I was so glad for the extra money, I didn't know I'd feel like this." Marie was silent. "I don't know what I'll do." Bruce seemed unsure and then brightened up when he said, "Maybe I'll talk with Eric, the supervisor, in parts. He got promoted last year."

"Yes," Marie said, "that will give you some important information." Marie thought about inviting Eric and his wife over for dinner but decided to wait to see if Bruce followed up on his plan. She just smiled and thought, *What a healthy way to go*.

Teeter-tottering Back and Forth

By focusing on Bruce's emotions, Marie encouraged Bruce not only to recognize, label, and accept his feelings but to move on to other thoughts, feelings, and plans. People on tilt, who have ambivalent feelings, get pushed both forward and backward. Bruce wanted to go forward in his new position, but he also wanted to go backward to his buddies.

Bruce was able to put his feelings into words, but not everyone can. Many people deny, ignore, or minimize their ambivalent feelings.

Practicing active listening enables us to reflect not only the emotions that the person describes but also those ambivalent ones that we sense from the way he acts or the way he talks about an event. If his body language contradicts his words, we need to check it out. We can use disclaimers such as "It looks like" and "I'm wondering if . . ." to share our impressions.

Once ambivalent feelings are accurately described and accepted, people become more comfortable with them. The information we share can help people who are tilting back and forth to regain their balance. We'll say more about that when we talk about feedback in Chapter 22.

Elaine's Listening Lesson

Elaine, a hard-driving executive, was pleased but concerned when Connie, a close friend, asked to get together to talk over coffee rather than to go shopping, as they did most weekends. Connie sounded upset.

Elaine knew that Connie and her boyfriend, Bob, a recovering alcoholic, were having problems. As they sipped coffee, Connie began crying. Between sobs she explained that after eight years Bob had met her demands and finally "gotten sober," but she still wanted to leave him. Elaine did everything she could to comfort her. Connie stopped crying and listened to her suggestions, but then she didn't speak with Elaine or return her calls for almost three months.

Elaine explained to us that what she learned from this experience was something her mother told her: "Connie didn't want advice, she wanted you to listen. Next time just listen." After talking with her mom, Elaine felt worse. Although her mother was partly right, she wasn't a model of good listening herself. So Elaine came to our workshop to learn some new skills.

Guilt Traps Can Immobilize

Connie was ambivalent about Bob's recovery and needed to sort through her own feelings. When the couple argued, Bob would yell, "I finally get help and now you want to leave me. You never really wanted me to recover." Bob's guilt trap was immobilizing Connie.

If Elaine had avoided advice and taken time to ask about her feelings, Connie probably would have gotten in touch with several emotions. She might have sorted through her sadness about the seven earlier years, the hurt she felt when Bob accused her of not wanting him to recover, her scary confusion about the mixed feelings she had, as well as the guilt that Bob's accusation generated. By expressing these feelings and labeling them, Connie probably would have been freed up to sort through her options.

When Elaine learned about the A question, she recognized how valuable it could have been and looked forward to using it. She also realized how ambivalent she had felt about her mother's advice. Elaine appreciated learning what she did wrong. She also recognized how frustrated she was when her mom didn't help her solve her own problems by looking at her options. Realizing how well she had handled her own situation, she began to see the benefits of going through the steps of H.E.A.L.T.H.Y. when there was no one there to help her. Elaine and others have taught us the versatility of these methods, particularly for the self-help discussed earlier.

A Deeper Exploration of the Emotional Terrain

There are many ways of mapping emotions, but other than the simplest Mad, Sad, and Glad, most maps come down to about four to six major feelings. The map we presented in Chapter 9 is reprinted here. The states on our map include Happy, Sad, Angry, Hurt, and Afraid. In addition, some emotions are at the juncture of two, three, or even four states.

Happy	Sad	Angry	Hurt	Afraid
Committed	Ashamed	Annoyed	Abandoned	Anxious
Determined	Blue	Bitter	Deceived	Bashful
Excited	Defeated	Bored	Embarrassed	Doubtful
Fantastic	Depressed	Bothered	Empty	Frightened
Good	Disappointed	Confused	Foolish	Intimidated
Grateful	Down	Enraged	Left Out	Overextended
Great	Embarrassed	Impatient	Lonely	Powerless
Optimistic	Empty	Infuriated	Needy	Pressured
Passionate	Hopeless	Irritated	Pained	Scared
Pleased	Miserable	Mad	Tired	Suspicious
Relieved	Sorry	Resentful	Tortured	Uncertain
Surprised	Tired	Trapped		Upset
Thrilled	Worthless			Weak
				Worried

Notice in the flat map above that the elevations in the five emotional states are not shown because they are listed alphabetically rather than by intensity. When people pass through a state, however, they do so at different levels of emotional intensity. If we can find the level that they are experiencing and reflect it back to them, they will feel more deeply understood than if we had used a flat map to describe their emotional landscape.

To enhance our ability to reflect feelings accurately, we may want to vary elevations in each emotional state. The map below presents three different elevations for each of the five major emotional categories.

HAPPY	SAD	ANGRY	HURT	AFRAID
Fantastic	Miserable	Enraged	Tortured	Terrified
Great	Depressed	Mad	Pained	Scared
Good	Disappointed	Irritated	Embarrassed	Worried

Name That Emotion and Its Intensity

To enhance our ability to pinpoint the right feeling at the right intensity, we may want to practice expressing our own emotions to someone at least once a day. It is best to simply explain this goal to someone trustworthy and then regularly tell that person, "I feel ____." Not only will this enhance our empathic abilities, it will probably bring us even closer to the person we've chosen.

If we are working with a partner who is also learning to use the H.E.A.L.T.H.Y. way, we may want to play "Name That Feeling." One of us describes a feeling or uses body language to express it. The other one tries to guess what it is.

With practice we'll come to know the emotional terrain quite well. We'll have our own, internal typographic map with a growing number of twists, turns, and nuances of emotions, as well as their many rolling hills, valleys, and elevations.

In the next chapter we will explore the thoughts and beliefs that make us each unique and that underlie most of the emotional upheavals that put us on tilt.

2 1

Tapping Their Thinking

"The meaning of a message is half said and half heard."

—AUTHOR UNKNOWN

Jeannie has been divorced for less than two years. She is living with her nine-year-old daughter in a house that she still owns jointly with George, her former husband. Frank, the lawyer who handled the divorce, was pleasantly surprised by the friendly and cooperative manner in which Jeannie and George were able to end their marriage.

Recently Jeannie set up several appointments with Frank to discuss selling the house, but repeatedly canceled them at the last minute. Frustrated by her cancellations, Frank wonders if child-custody problems are surfacing.

When Jeannie arrives, Frank notices that she seems nervous. She has trouble sitting still and shifts uneasily in the chair.

Frank just learned the H.E.A.L.T.H.Y. technique in a workshop and decides to put it to the test. He asks, "Jeannie, what's happening in your life?"

"I just got engaged and my new boyfriend has moved into the house," Jeannie discloses.

"How do you feel about that?"

"I'm very excited," Jeannie answers, adding, "It's nice to finally find a man who loves me."

Frank moves to A and asks, "Any other feelings?"

"Well," Jeannie hesitates, "now that you mention it, I'm a little worried because we've been having a lot of fights lately. Sometimes I think I have a talent for drawing difficult men into my life."

Having listened very carefully, Frank reflects back to Jeannie, "Looks like you're excited and worried at the same time about your engagement."

"You're right about that," Jeannie responds.

Going on to T, Frank asks, "What troubles you the most?"

"Well, my fiancé is very critical of my divorce settlement," says Jeannie, "and he keeps bugging me to stop being nice to my ex-husband."

Not sure where the conversation is going, Frank follows the steps to H and asks, "How are you handling that?"

Jeannie sighs. "That's what all the fighting's about."

Turning to Y, Frank looks for a way to say yes. Looking directly and warmly at Jeannie, he says, "Yes, I can understand that you'd be upset. I'm so glad you came to see me. Let's look at the divorce settlement again. What would you like me to do?"

As Jeannie's shoulders relax, she leans back in her chair and says, "The divorce settlement is fine. I think I just need you to explain it to my fiancé. Maybe I need to sell the house and buy a new house with him. I need your advice on a lot of stuff."

At this point Frank feels terrific. Jeannie's needs for legal counsel are now clear and manageable. As her lawyer he may be able to avoid the rough closing that so often accompanies the sale of a home after a divorce. Frank is also coming to understand better what his favorite professor had called the essential second part of a license that reads, "Attorney and *Counselor* at Law."

The Power of Meaning

Earlier, when Frank tried to make sense out of the canceled appointments, he misunderstood their meaning as related to child custody. By using the "What's happening" question Frank could avoid both implying that George and Jeannie were having custody problems and putting Jeannie on the defensive. He also saved time.

Even if Frank had started by asking, "What brings you here today?" Jeannie might have taken a lot longer getting to the real problem. Without the "Any other feelings?" question she might have been stuck in her ambivalence over her new relationship. Without the "What troubles you most?" question, Jeannie might have gotten a review of her divorce settlement, but shied away from either sharing or discovering her need for Frank to explain the settlement to her fiancé. In this case these two powerful questions, about feelings and thoughts, probably averted a second meeting with still more cancellations.

Stress Is in the Eye of the Beholder

Clarifying the thoughts behind people's words, feelings, and actions yields many exciting benefits. It helps us to connect in meaningful ways, not only in our professional and work associations but also in our most intimate relationships.

The primary cause of divorce is probably, as Groucho Marx quipped, marriage; but the stress of misunderstood meanings is a very close second. Stress, as well as beauty, is in the eye and the mind of the beholder.

Remember, stress is the body's fight-flight-or-freeze response to anything *believed* to be dangerous, disappointing, or demanding. This belief is the sum total of our unique life experiences and our singular ways of thinking up to that moment. These thoughts create our private worlds. They are the stories that we tell ourselves about the way things are. This is why the meaning and stress of any event for a given individual simply cannot be predicted or understood without asking for the person's story.

A couple struggling to make increasingly short ends meet, for example, receives a major financial gift from one of their parents. As the woman cries with joy and hugs her husband, he is quiet and distant. In the morning they fight over what she wants to spend on the children's Christmas presents. The meaning of the money they received is quite different for the wife and the husband. Only if she asks or he tells her will she be able to listen attentively and learn what made him go on tilt.

Two people from the same town and religious and ethnic background who marry may still discover that their expectations of how a husband and wife are "supposed" to relate are very different. This is particularly true in teen marriages, where both partners are growing and changing as rapidly as the latest hairstyle. Premarital counseling, involving a review of the expectations about a wide range of future plans, can be extremely valuable in uncovering these differences. If counseling is not available, important questions for the partners to answer alone and together include "What troubles you the most about our relationship?" and "What are your most cherished expectations about our relationship?" Each person's horror-movie fantasies and fairy-tale endings need to be spoken and heard.

People talk about the importance of good communication in marriage, but most aren't quite sure what it means. To improve communication when one partner is stressed-out, the other must find out what specifically troubles the partner about the situation. When both understand what it means to the other, then they have communicated.

One Change, Many Meanings

How differently each person sees and thinks about the same event became clear when one of us—the one with options about facial hair—shaved off his beard. His son advised against change and his daughter couldn't wait to see it. Once the deed was done, the son thought he looked like a baseball player and loved watching him shave. The daughter, on the other hand, thought it looked awful and hated the feel of "sandpaper" on his face. His mother-in-law, who wouldn't unlock the door to her house, said later, "I never thought I'd live to see it." It is clear that the beard meant something different to each of these people.

When the clean-shaven face appeared at work, the reactions were equally diverse. One patient said that he was cuter but not as distinguished, while the very next one said that he looked much *more* distinguished. Several patients and co-workers wondered how he "grew" a moustache so quickly.

What about the author's own thoughts? When people looked at him strangely, he learned how automatically he still thinks *What did I do wrong?* before focusing on *What about me or the situation troubles them?* Life is a wonderful teacher.

Hypochondriasis Hits a Crowd

In Monterey Park, California, a sellout crowd was enjoying a great football game, when they heard over the loudspeaker, "May we have your attention? Please do not drink the soda from our food stands. Several people had already come down with what appears to be a form of food poisoning resulting from old copper piping." Moments earlier a physician had been summoned to examine three dizzy, nauseated fans and advised the management to make the announcement. Within minutes hundreds of fans were fainting from dizziness and throwing up from nausea. Over two hundred left to seek medical care as five ambulances raced to and from nearby hospitals.

By halftime those in charge had spoken with relatives and discovered that all three of the original patients must have eaten spoiled food elsewhere, and an announcement was made that the soda was safe to drink. The fans who had felt nauseated but hadn't thrown up soon felt better, and probably never realized how they had demonstrated that thoughts alone can cause and cure illness.

Words and images, as well as the thoughts and beliefs they symbolize, affect not only our health but also our strength. Researchers used an exercise machine to measure the leg strength of thirty-six women, twenty-four of whom spent twenty minutes a day for three days contracting their thigh muscles but *only in their imagination*. The mental exercise increased leg strength by over 12 percent. Those who did not think about contracting their leg muscles showed no changes. Surely if thoughts alone can strengthen muscles, we must respect their power to affect our reality.

Concentration Camps and the Importance of Meaning

Shakespeare wrote in Hamlet, "There is nothing good or bad, but thinking makes it so." What about the brutality of a concentration camp? Given the same inhumane conditions, some people are able to hold on, while others give up and perish. In *Man's Search for Meaning* Victor Frankl described his triumph over evil by finding significance in his suffering and wrote, "To live is to suffer, to survive is to find meaning in the suffering."

There Are Usually at Least Two Sides to Each Experience

When Michael's brother joined the army, he told one of us that he dreaded his mother's reaction. Michael said he knew that he'd try to explain to his mother why his brother had to leave and try to convince her that it was all for the best, but she'd still be upset for days. Interested in doing something more effective, he was excited about using H.E.A.L.T.H.Y.

Late that night, when he tried to ask her, "What troubles you the most?" he mistakenly asked, "What thrills you most?" His mother responded quickly that she'd get the back rent he owed her. They both laughed. She then explained that he wanted her to pay his bills, so he had given her permission to cosign on his bank account. She was just going to make sure hers got paid first!

What's the Bottom Line?

Giving people a chance to sort through their thoughts about a change frees them up to respond more effectively and move on to new experiences. This is particularly important today because everything is changing more rapidly than ever before.

When we are absorbed by violence in the news, a controversial community issue, or job insecurity, we feel threatened and find it difficult to focus on creative solutions to challenging new problems. Those negative thoughts constitute our reality.

When we are preoccupied at work with thoughts about a loved one in the hospital or a child in trouble, it's like listening to a portable CD player that's stuck on a single selection. The same is true when we are thinking about something wonderful like winning the lottery or getting engaged, even if we think that the change will make all our problems go away. In either case it's hard to reach us with new information and it's hard for us to learn new job skills.

As Mary Kay Ash, president and founder of Mary Kay Cosmetics, says, "Just how far a manager should go in discussing an employee's personal problems is something only the individuals involved can determine." Many managers find that when they help an employee specify the thoughts that under-

lie their reactions to a stressful situation, they free them up to
work more effectively.

Research with over 2,399 employees of a large corporation
showed that families take more hits from job stress than jobs
take from family stress. Satisfaction with parenting was most
closely related to having an employer who was supportive of
the employees' emerging family needs.

In the long run, providing emotional support on the job is
likely to retain more workers than any combination of raises,
bonuses, and benefits. Getting involved with employees builds
a trusting and productive environment. Ultimately, as James A.
Autry writes in *Love and Profit,* "If you're not creating community, you're not managing."

Peeling the Onion Without Tears

Do you make your living by selling? It can be argued that
we all sell something, so regardless of your answer, you will
probably appreciate what Mike McNight points out: "People
don't really care how much you know until they know how
much you care."

Asking what troubles or thrills people the most about their
problems or our products will give us valuable information and
will let them know we care about them as people.

Gwen, a realtor, learned this when she was showing an attractive apartment to a young woman named Sue. As they entered the master bedroom, Gwen wanted Sue to visualize
living in the home and asked, "Do you and your partner prefer
a king- or a queen-sized bed?"

Unexpectedly Sue began to cry. Gwen asked her what was
going on in her life and learned that Sue's husband had died
of cancer just six months before. Their bed had been a very
special place for Sue and Bob, as it is for most couples. Sue
feared her painful loneliness would never end. Gwen couldn't
see Sue's emotional wounds, but they were festering just the
same.

When asked what about the move troubled her the most, Sue responded that it meant giving up their house, their hopes for the future, and really admitting that Bob was gone. Gwen was able to empathize by saying, "Yes, I can see that it would be very difficult for you. It really means you are starting over by yourself."

Certainly if Gwen had known, she would never have asked Sue that sales question in that particular way. However, once she knew about the problem, she was able to connect in a positive way. She could also tailor the information she gave Sue and avoid overloading her mind. Gwen respected Sue's limits and helped her find a suitable apartment. Looking back, Gwen wished that she'd learned about H.E.A.L.T.H.Y. communications earlier and looked forward to using it with all her clients.

Regardless of our occupation, we all have the opportunity to deal caringly or coldly with stressed-out people. We can ignore, reject, or connect with their experience. The choices and the results are ours.

Aha! Theirs and Ours

Ever wonder if asking others to think about a problem will only increase their preoccupation? Fortunately just the opposite is true. It takes energy to keep from worrying about "outside" thoughts. When we are asked about our feelings and thoughts, this energy is freed up, and the stage is set for personal growth. It's far better to face our inner fears than to remain hostage to an outside force.

Our awareness of people's struggles and support of their efforts to cope conveys our sincere desire to be of service. If they think they can't do anything about a problem, our questions may lead them to view it differently. Even if no new actions are planned, when we connect and help people to shed new light on the meaning of their problems, it will ease their burdens and make our work more effective.

Every time we learn more about others, we also learn more

about ourselves. There is far more that unites us than divides us. The opportunities for personal growth and fulfillment are everywhere for everyone. Winston Churchill was right: "We make a living by what we get, but we make a life by what we give."

22

How to Stop Nagging
and Start Giving Feedback

*"None of us are saints, it seems,
but seeing there's no choice, . . .
I love you as a sinner even more."*
—BOB FRANKE

When Agnes began describing her husband, Carl, her body tensed, her mouth tightened, and her eyes narrowed. "It really annoys me the way he lets people walk all over him. Carl never stands up for himself. He's always doing something extra at work, staying late, and going in on Saturdays. I keep telling him that he should make other people pull their weight, but he doesn't listen to me."

Agnes is an unhappy lady. Carl doesn't live up to her expectations, and the more she lets him know it, the more each of them gets stressed-out. He's battered by her demands to change, and she's frustrated by his refusal.

Who Says They Shouldn't Do What They're Doing?

Regardless of how long we've lived, as folk singer Bob Franke says, "we've [all] been known, each in our own way, to be jerks." At any given time we can only be who and where we are in life.

By definition, being human means being imperfect. It also means that each of us has a right to decide what form that imperfection takes and how we are going to be in the world. For the most part we get to choose what we do and with whom we do it. Hopefully we will learn something in the process.

Does this mean that we have to stand idly by and watch someone we love self-destruct? Are we helpless? Shouldn't we influence those we care about to make some constructive changes in their lives? Can't we communicate our concern without diminishing their freedom?

It is always hard for people to hear criticism. "Constructive" or not, criticisms undermine relationships. Regardless of how we phrase it, people hear, "You are not okay."

Feedback Is Information

In the early days of guided missiles, scientists aimed a rocket at a target and then followed its trajectory. Using radio signals, they informed the missile's guidance system of its location in space and allowed it to correct its course and thereby reach its target. The information provided was called feedback. The scientists "fed back" information that the missile could use to correct for circumstances that caused it to stray from its predetermined path.

Feedback Helps People Get Where They Want to Go

The people in our lives all have some sense of where they want to go, what they want to do, and how they want to feel along the way. When we ask H.E.A.L.T.H.Y. questions, they can examine and express their thoughts and feelings in the face of the latest differences between what is and what they hoped for.

Sometimes our view of their situation is not the same as

their view of their situation. Often their behavior creates obstacles for us that make our paths more difficult. In either case we can ask them if they would like some feedback. If they do, we can share our view of what is happening.

When we provide feedback, it is important to report only objective information from what we observe. We need to allow the other person to determine whether the behavior described is helping them reach *their* goals.

Levels of Feedback

Most people do not like to be confronted with negative information about themselves. We all have ways of blocking out things we do not want to hear. Therefore the more neutral our reports, the more likely other people are to hear them. In addition, when offering feedback, it is important to ask, "Is this a good time to talk?" It may not be. If people are overwhelmed, they cannot process new information. Even if they could process it, they may not want to. Feedback should never be imposed. Assuming they want to talk, we can prepare them for our gifts by asking, "Would you like some feedback?" Most feedback can be postponed.

Level-one feedback is simply a statement of what we observed. The more specific, the better. Agnes avoids telling Carl what to do, for example. She simply comments that he has rarely been getting home until after eight P.M. and he's been going to work for at least five hours on Saturdays. A shorter alternative here for level-one feedback would be "You look tired." Once the feedback is expressed, the other person can decide if he or she wants to do anything about it.

Feedback is a gift. It gives other people information that they can either use or ignore. It does not demand a response.

Gifts of feedback can come in small as well as large packages. If a child's shoelace is untied, we might turn our eyes to her shoes and say, "It looks like you have a flat tire."

Level-two feedback gives additional information, specifically our reaction to the person's behavior. Unless we focus on how we feel and then share our feelings, the information is not available. Without it people do not understand the impact of their behavior on others. Once they understand how their behavior affects us, they may wish to change their course. This is why feedback about our reaction is such worthwhile information for those around us.

Agnes would be giving Carl level-two feedback if she says, "When you come home so late, I miss your company. I love looking forward to seeing you and having dinner with you." Agnes's gift is information about her feelings about his behavior. Carl, and only Carl, gets to decide whether he wants to accept the gift or do anything about it. This is very different from the global, judgmental demands most of us typically make of other people.

Level-three feedback is when we describe someone's behavior and then tell the person what we think might be the consequences. This, too, can be valuable information. Agnes might say, "If you continue to spend so much time at work, I am going to have to find something to occupy me. Then I may not be available when you want to do something with me." Said neutrally, this is not a threat. Agnes is simply offering information to Carl for his consideration. It is likely to shed new light on what might happen if he continues to spend time at work and not at home.

Pull, Don't Push

Feedback works best when we include some positive aspects of the person's behavior and use the minimum possible level of feedback. If a level-one observation will do the job, for example, it is far more effective than making a level-three guess about what the future might bring.

Feedback is information. What people do with it is up to them. When we give feedback, we must respect people's right to make their own decisions. We simply give them our information. We hope the feedback will help them to make wise decisions, but making those decisions must be left entirely up to them.

The positive parts of the message about their behavior and our relationship are essential. Why? People only change when they want to change. So if we want people to change, there's got to be something in it for them.

What if we maintain that they *must* make a change? In general the more we push other people to change their behavior, the more they will resist. People can and will change, but only if and when they are ready to change.

The Power of Specific Feedback

Recently we were asking people how they had applied their new knowledge about different levels of feedback. One of the first to respond was Katherine. She enthusiastically reported that level two was "marvelous." We asked her to be more specific, since we believe that the best feedback speaks to specific behaviors rather than global labels.

Katherine looked embarrassed. The woman sitting next to her smiled encouragingly and urged, "Please tell us." Katherine blushed to the roots of her hair. "It's really personal," she said. The room was silent. With all eyes upon her Katherine consented, "Oh, all right," and blurted out, "For years I have been trying to get my husband to put the toilet seat down when he is through in the bathroom. He never listened. Maybe he didn't think it was a big deal and just expected me to adjust. Anyway we had a lot of knock-down, drag-out fights about it.

"Last week," she continued, "I finally got him to hear me. All I said was, 'It feels so awful, in the middle of the night, when I put my bare butt on that cold, wet seat.' I don't think he ever realized how uncomfortable it made me feel. He hasn't slipped up since. And I haven't slipped down either!" The volume of cheers and applause suggested that she was not alone and that a lot of husbands were about to get some clear feedback at whatever level it took to bring about change.

What can we do if we witness something as serious as a stranger hitting a child? This is a very difficult situation, but one in which we may still be of some help, short of calling Child Protection Services. Hopefully the abuse is a rare loss of control. "Dear Abby" advises, "Very gently and quietly attempt to calm the person by saying, '. . . Sometimes taking a child that age shopping is more than we can handle.' "

Why Nagging Doesn't Work

Stressed-out people are especially sensitive to being corrected, scolded, or otherwise found lacking. When we want to help other people change their behavior, nagging seldom succeeds.

Once we've told a smoker, for example, that he is important to us and that we don't like smoke getting between us, it's time to back off. We can remind him that he's conquered other challenges in the past, we can agree that it's a gripping addiction, and we can offer our support, but after that it's up to him. Otherwise he may agree with George Burns, who says, "Happiness is having a large, loving, caring, close-knit family . . . in another city."

Why is nagging so counterproductive? Repeated advice only diminishes others. Our judgments are put-downs. People often feel that we must think we're more practical, clever, and experienced than they.

Nagging is also unproductive because it serves up a large portion of guilt to heap on their already overflowing plate. Guilt traps can immobilize. If anything, we want to alleviate guilt in order to foster movement.

In addition to fostering guilt and ill will, nagging communicates the opposite of respect. It only adds to the painful doubts we all have about ourselves and our sometimes-deep feelings of insecurity. Our behavior may be self-defeating and even self-destructive, but before we can change, we must believe our self is worth saving.

Sometimes people say, "I want to change, but I can't." Isn't there anything we can do to help? That's where feedback comes in. There is an old adage: "People are not weak—they're just not in touch with their power." Using feedback, we can help them rediscover their strengths. We can provide information that will encourage them to focus on their abilities rather than their deficiencies. We can share our positive feelings.

To increase their sense of power, we might respond to "I can't" with "Up till now you have found it difficult."

The Proof Is in "Peanuts"

Let's see how Charles Schultz illustrates the downside risks of nagging in "Peanuts." Lucy, who compensates for her own low self-esteem with a know-it-all attitude, asks Linus if he'd like her to remind him of all his faults. When Linus replies that he definitely would not, Lucy exclaims, "See? Right there is one of your problems. You have no desire to improve."

Linus shouts back, "I DON'T NEED YOU TO HELP ME IMPROVE." Undaunted, Lucy persists, "And you're so impatient! You get upset so easily."

Linus retreats, which prompts Lucy to point out that "storming out of the room" is no solution. Her final shot? Lucy reminds him that he failed to turn off the TV before leaving the room.

We are on Linus's side. We don't think it is our job to help people to "improve."

Catch Them Doing Something Positive

As a supervisor or manager at work, our job may be to help people improve and fulfill their job requirements. In this case everything we said about nagging also applies to management by criticism. If we are up-front with clear goals and allow the people who work with us to help create those goals, no manipulation is involved when we recognize and reward steps toward those goals.

This approach is also useful in the home with young children and in the classroom. One gifted teacher was able to change the "personality" of an elementary class from negative to positive by focusing the children's attention on the "good" rather than the "bad" in their classmates and encouraging them to "catch others when they are being helpful." We can all benefit by looking for the good in one another and sharing what we find.

Another excellent teacher gave the following level-two feedback: "I noticed that you took care to help Johnnie with his boots, and that really made me feel good." This kind of feedback allows children to feel the impact of doing something kind for others. It builds self-esteem.

The Pitfalls of Praise

Problems can arise, however, when people apply this when they are not supervising, teaching, or parenting. Approval from others can actually *diminish* our freedom. Think about it. Praise can lock you into behavior. Changing would then risk losing love and approval.

Most relationships are or can become relationships between equals. Praise is usually based on our goals rather than the other person's goals. In more democratic relationships an alternative to praise might be "Looks like you're doing more of what you wanted to do. I'm glad." When someone relates an accomplishment, we may choose to reflect, "Sounds like you feel very good about that."

Arguments about how someone should feel or act cannot be won. When we make the other person "wrong," everyone loses. The losses include lowered self-esteem, increased resentment, and diminished trust. As I. Cheureux wrote, "A friend is someone who leaves you with all your freedom intact but who, by what he thinks of you, obliges you to be fully what you are."

Can we communicate to people that we'll accept "whatever floats your boat," when it looks like they're about to hit a reef and drown? After all, sometimes we're all in the same boat, sinking. What if a teenager, for example, is making a big mistake? Trying to protect people from the natural consequences of trial-and-error learning expresses a lack of faith in their basic ability to learn.

Alternatives to Warning and Resenting

It is useful, however, to ask them what their assessment is of the best and worst possible outcomes of their behavior. If in spite of this they still chose a risky path, unless there is clear physical danger, it is important to let them learn from their decisions.

In any case we can assure them that we will continue to be there for them regardless of what happens. We can also suggest that things will not get worse by telling us what's happening in their life and that even if they make mistakes, we believe in their ability to recover. We can help keep them afloat so that they don't drown, but they will only swim toward land when it represents something they want. There is much wisdom in the old Zen saying "The raft is not the shore."

What sort of things can we do while people are hanging on our raft? To help others rebound and learn, we might ask some very positive questions, such as "How are you going to make things better?" or "How will you know when you are out of the woods?" or "What do you really want?"

If the person has taken us off our path, what can we do after we've done all we can to get back on our path? To avoid judging what they've done to us and wasting energy on our hurt, anger, and revenge, we can move on to the next adventure on our path. How? As Peter McWilliams says, "Forgiving and forgetting makes you available *for giving* and *for getting.*"

"You Cannot Expect Change Without Changing"

To get others to change, we may need to change our own behavior. Lonely children, for example, need our help to establish friendships. The problems of the withdrawn child are often overlooked at school because teachers attend first to the most disruptive children. Sometimes we can teach children social skills and get them involved with others through organized activities. In addition, parents may need to look in the mirror and see if they have become so focused on the child's problem that they have withdrawn from their own adult activities. If so, they need to change in order to give the child a model of cooperative and playful involvement with others.

It may also be useful to ask children for feedback. What do they see us doing to try to get them to conform to our image of how they should be. How does our pushing make them feel? This information will most likely make us want to change our behavior.

Let's take some other examples. Parents who smoke, chew gum, or overeat may need to realize how their habits relate to the behaviors of their children, from thumb-sucking to preoccupations with food. We can provide feedback for ourselves. Once we discover how what we do relates to the problem, we can begin leading the way by accepting ourselves and giving up our security blankets.

This is difficult work, but for a variety of reasons, change invites change. First, seeing another person change inspires hope that change is possible. Second, the one who chooses to make the first change realizes just how hard change can be and becomes more accepting. This is especially true for those of us in marriages where we want our partners to change but we may need to change first.

The Cycles of Change

Psychologists studying the way people change addictive behaviors have shown that there are several stages of change, and most people cycle through them a number of times before the change is permanent. In smoking cessation, for example, people typically attempt to quit three or four times before succeeding.

Some people are not convinced of the need to change. Without feedback or other information, they will remain stuck in the cycle and simply go through the motions, over and over again.

Ultimately the *contemplative* stage of the cycle is the most crucial. This is where people must recognize that *they* want to change, or else the change will be fleeting. Positive level-one or level-two feedback, in the absence of nagging, can help further the process. In addition, time to think it through and really get used to the idea is another helpful gift. At this point we need to give people space. It can't be ours; it's got to be theirs.

The Silent Gift

To support someone who is changing, we can avoid nagging and give them the silent gift of touch. As we will see in the next chapter, a pat on the back, a hug, or a smile often communicates our caring and our faith in people far louder than words.

23

Touching Is Good Contact

Hugs are better than drugs

Imagine that everyone around you has been screaming all afternoon and has wanted everything right away. It's late now, and you haven't eaten since lunchtime. You're feeling worn and irritable as you fight your way home along the rainy freeway.

Think about dinner. Which would you prefer, fast-food take-out in a noisy car or a home-cooked meal with familiar voices? Which would comfort you more, crawling into bed and pulling the covers over your head or being held and stroked by someone who cares? Silly questions? Probably. But the point we are trying to make is that human contact, specifically being touched, is essential to our sense of well-being. And that means both our physical and our psychological well-being.

More than half the orphans in an early-twentieth-century French institution wasted away every year until doctors discovered why some of the infants were doing well while others were dying. All the infants were receiving basic care, but it was the equivalent of eating fast food alone in your car. The nurses handled the infants only as much as necessary to get the work done. On one ward, however, the nurses routinely touched, held, and snuggled the infants. Those infants deprived of touch became depressed, seriously ill, and often died, but those infants receiving regular cuddling thrived.

In the United States, well into the twentieth century, nearly all the infants in foundling institutions died before they reached the age of one year for lack of tender, loving care (TLC). Then a study at Bellevue Hospital in New York City found that handling, carrying, caressing, and cuddling infants, even in the absence of much else, cut mortality rates to less than 10 percent. The critical factor? Touch.

The When, Where, and Whom of Touch

It is sad that we have learned so little from these studies. Yes, we provide more touch to hospitalized infants, but otherwise healthy children and adults continue to suffer needlessly from skin hunger. We all need more TLC than most of us get. And touch is basic to TLC.

The skin is the largest organ of the body. In addition the largest surface of our brains is dedicated to receiving impulses from the skin. When we are hungry for skin contact, we often substitute overeating, drinking, and drugging to satisfy our craving. Skin hunger increases our level of stress. Studies show that people who are the most uncomfortable with touch have lower self-esteem, more anxiety, and poorer body images. Other than in athletic competition and children's play, we seldom see touching in public. On television we see extremes, with more hitting and kissing than hugging or touching.

What keeps us from initiating and enjoying the close encounters we so desperately need? In our culture touch may be the communication channel that we most carefully program and self-consciously regulate.

We learn about touch in our earliest years. Studying children from two to five years of age and their caretakers in what was then the Soviet Union, as well as in Greece and America, psychologists found that American parents soothed, held, and touched significantly less while playing with their children than did parents from the other countries. No wonder we have bumper stickers that ask us HAVE YOU HUGGED YOUR CHILD TO-DAY?

As adults talking with friends in a restaurant over a cup of coffee, Americans touch one another on average twice an hour, while our counterparts in France touch 110 times an hour and in Puerto Rico, 180 times. Only friends in England touch less, and they hardly make any physical contact. Some say that our Puritan heritage makes it difficult for us to become comfortable with touch. Just as cultures vary, so do the sexes.

The Gender Gap

Not surprisingly a study of airplane travelers demonstrated that women touch, kiss, and embrace far longer and more often than men, who are more likely simply to shake hands.

Only in sports, it seems, can men openly hug and touch one another without raising issues of homosexuality. Studying swimmers, researchers found that regardless of sex, the winners get six times more touches than the losers, who might be much more in need of support.

Surprisingly men touched by a nurse giving them information before major surgery responded with increases in blood pressure and anxiety, whereas women in the same situation relaxed as a result of physical contact by the nurse. The meanings of touch, and thus the responses to touch, are different for everyone.

Gender differences were dramatized beautifully in the movie *Annie Hall*, when Woody Allen and Diane Keaton were each asked by their therapists about the frequency with which they made love. His answer? "Hardly ever, maybe three times a week." Hers? "Constantly, three times a week."

Watch Your Boundaries

If this is such a "touchy" issue, wouldn't it be safest to avoid physical contact with stressed-out people? Men and women who are completely uncomfortable with touch, regardless of sex, do tend to be emotionally unstable, rigidly authoritarian, or socially withdrawn. But most of us do not have personality disorders; we are more or less stable people who are under stress and temporarily go on tilt. Often a comforting pat on the back or a firm hand on a shoulder can help us realize that we are not as isolated and vulnerable as we feel.

According to Richard Heslin, Ph.D., of Purdue University, the touches we give are dependent on our roles and our relationships, and they fall into five, prescribed categories. *Professional* touches are infrequent and free of personal messages. *Social* touches include handshakes, and these are limited to hellos, good-byes and thank-yous. *Friendly* touches are exchanged between neighbors and co-workers, for example. *Love* touches are confined to family members and close friends. *Sexual* touches are the most intimate and highly charged.

We would like to promote an increase in the third category, friendly touches, across all five types of relationships.

The Meaning of Touch

A friend calls you on your birthday. An acquaintance remembers your interest in a particular subject. You are touched. Symbolically that means a warm, caring gesture has been received.

Stressed-out people are often so preoccupied with the things that bother them that it is hard to reach them. The phone companies are right when they suggest that we should reach out and touch somebody. It is a way to make contact and communicate caring. Our popular music echoes the same themes. "I want to hold your hand," "Lean on me," and "Put your head on my shoulder" are all ways of saying, "I care about you and I want to help." We send strong messages of support when we use our hands to make physical contact in nonthreatening ways.

Traffic Lights

As with the levels of feedback, it is best to stay low and go slow with touch, so as not to be misunderstood. We only have a green light to touch if someone asks us to touch; otherwise the light is always yellow and we must proceed with caution. Even a slight stiffening is a dangerous sign and should be treated like a red light.

Touch influences us in many powerful ways. It is harder, for example, to refuse someone who touches us. Studies have shown that librarians who brush the hands of patrons when returning library cards improve attitudes toward the library; and waiters who touch their customer's hand or shoulder when returning change receive more of it back in tips. The next time you are mad at someone close to you, try something new. Hold hands and look directly into each other's eyes while talking about your grievances. This kind of touch also strengthens the positive impact of feedback.

Research shows that the right to touch is in the hands of those with power. Politicians shake hands and kiss babies to connect and get votes. Touchers are higher on the human pecking order and have more power than the touched. This brings up the potential for abuse and the importance of using touch with the highest integrity.

Research shows that when therapists touch their patients, patients see them as more expert. This is important because it increases trust and helps people to share their deepest concerns. Through taped sessions reviewed and judged by other researchers, it was found that those patients who were touched by their therapist explored deeper issues sooner than those who were untouched. When someone touches us, we feel accepted.

Why Not Just Ask?

People vary widely in their comfort zones for touch. We need to respect these differences. Most of us, however, when faced with some new and difficult situation, appreciate someone "holding our hand" while we struggle to achieve some sense of mastery.

Touch can send a valuable message of support to anyone, anywhere, at any time. To our buddies in the trenches of life, a pat on the back, a caring hug, or some direct eye contact with a smile can all say, "I'm glad you're here with me." Friends may not know how to ask for touch. If so, it may be best to ask, "Can I give you a hand?" or "Would a back rub help?"

The Healing Touch

A gentle neck massage, a tender touch, or a meeting of our eyes are rapid stress relievers. Research shows that touch may not only comfort, it may cure.

Just petting a dog or cat lowers heart rate and blood pressure in both the petter *and* the pet. Scientists fed rabbits a very high-cholesterol diet under two conditions to study the effects of touch on heart disease. By petting, speaking, and playing with some of the rabbits the experimenters found that these rabbits developed significantly less atherosclerosis than rabbits given routine care. In another study, cancer cells injected into mice caged alone multiplied faster than the same cells injected into mice caged together. The sight, sound, and touch of another made a healthy difference.

Harry Harlow's landmark studies separating baby monkeys from their mothers found that those infants who were fed adequately but totally deprived of cuddling were unable to develop normally. As adults they became anxious, fearful, and sexually dysfunctional. In those cases where the youngsters were allowed physical contact with peers, their social and physical development appeared normal.

Dr. Dolores Krieger, professor of nursing at New York University, developed new methods of therapeutic touch to help heal patients. By "listening" with her hands as she scans the patient's body for tension, she attunes herself to the patient's tension, redirects that energy, and gives of her own excess energies in healing ways. Fancy terms such as *electron transfer resonance* now give new meaning to the ancient practice of laying on of hands.

Expanding Your ZIP Code

We all have comfort zones for touching and receiving touch. We can all place a higher priority on the delivery of these caring messages by taking a tip from the postal service and adding ZIP to our lives. The letters in *ZIP* stand for "Zone Improvement Plan." We can't wait passively for a touching delivery; it may never come.

Giving and receiving hugs or shoulder massages doesn't have to be a game of musical chairs or a complex obstacle course. We can start making these gestures part of our regular daily routine. Inviting our immediate world to touch us in specific ways that provide mutual pleasure can bridge the loneliness barrier and establish multiple channels for communication. Then we'll all be ready to provide relief when people get stressed-out.

We need to invent new forms of touch and closeness, such as the all-hands-on-deck family hug. These are the messages and the notes that can punctuate our lives with love. It's time to ask, guide, and thank those who touch us.

Change is always gradual, but with perseverance and patience we can all come in from the cold. With friendly touch we can give each other the personal warmth we all need.

In the next chapter we will explore ways of reaching out to others who have lost forever the touch of someone close to them.

24

Supporting Those
Struck by Tragedy

"Do not speak unless you can improve the silence."
—AUTHOR UNKNOWN

TWO SHOTS FIRED, TWO TEENS DEAD

SMALL TOWN, USA—Two local youths are dead, another is behind bars, and a fourth person is in critical condition at Small Memorial Hospital, following a robbery of the Main Street Pizza Shack and a high-speed car chase. Dead are . . .

The people named in the news story all have family, friends, and acquaintances. The tragedy touches all these lives. What do we say to the moms of these teens? What do we say to their school friends or to the husband of the bystander who was hit by the getaway car?

A tragedy does not have a simple solution. When people are just stressed-out, we can help them sort through their emotions and their options and can prompt the feelings of competence and connectedness. When people are in a major crisis

and experiencing serious loss, panic, or shock, as are those reacting to the drama reported above, we may find ourselves unsure of what to do, how to cope with their distress, or how to
provide emotional first aid. Actually the most supportive thing
that we can do is simply to be there. Not to do anything. Not
to say anything. They can't hear us anyway.

Things Shared Are Easier to Bear

Being there and, after a while, asking questions and seeking
the truth, communicates our faith that whatever has occurred,
the survivors will be strong enough to manage it. It also communicates in words and action that we are with them and that
we care. Being valued by others strengthens their self-esteem.

People in shock preserve their sanity by refusing to process
the event. Since they cannot yet acknowledge that anything
happened, they cannot yet feel anything. One of the moms of
the two dead teens in the newspaper story recalled, "It's terrible, it's like a state of shock. A few hours ago they were
watching TV with me. My son was falling asleep in the chair.
Then he told me they were going out and he was going to
spend the night at his friend's house."

Shutting Down with the Denial of Shock

When we receive bad news, most of us go into a protective
state of shock. The state comes in two parts: denial and numbness. At first we struggle with the news by denying it. We
don't believe it happened and we stop functioning. We need
people to be there for us, to help us deal with the details of
daily living and those related to the event. Later we will need
them to help us feel connected to other people and to the rest
of our lives that must go on. We will need them to help us feel
good about ourselves again. But now this is the time when we
must tell and retell the story.

We desperately need people to listen, not to avoid or change

the topic, but to listen. Only by repeating the story can we begin to believe it.

Lois Duncan, the mother of a teenage daughter who was
murdered in what police call a random shooting, explained this
need to *Women's Day* readers: "The people we found most
valuable of all were the ones who . . . encouraged Don and me
to talk about our nightmare experience and describe each ex-
cruciating detail over and over. That repetition diffused the intensity of our agony and made it possible for us to start the
healing process."

Avoidance

One open-faced question is usually all we need to ask.
"What happened?" works as well as any question. Some survivors may start but then hesitate, as if wondering if it's okay to
continue. It may help to touch their arm lightly and then ask,
"Would you like to tell me more about it?"

Giving survivors our undivided attention for short periods of
time is more valuable than half listening for a day. Often they
will seem to avoid questions or change the topic repeatedly.
People resist change and we all adjust to change at different
rates. It is important to be gentle with ourselves and with others. Most people need to absorb the realities of a crisis in
small doses.

It helps to check whether our questions have been moti-
vated by caring rather than curiosity. We don't want to cross-
examine survivors. Most of all, when they are ready to process
their experience, we want to be prepared to ask and find out
how they are doing.

Being There to Find the Truth

In helping people sort out what has happened, open-ended
questions are helpful. Reviewing the known is far less fright-

ening than speculating about the unknown. Fearful fantasies are far more terrifying than the truth.

Mothers with premature babies, for example, do best if they see their children as soon after birth as possible. This is even more important for the parents of a deformed or stillborn baby. Fortunately doctors and nurses are learning this, but most crises occur outside of hospitals, and we may need to encourage others to seek the truth. Such a search is a healthy way out of a crisis.

We live in a death-denying and death-avoidant society where most people die in hospitals rather than in their homes. There is a pornography of death in newspapers and movies, but for the most part we deny and avoid. Few of us have developed the skills necessary to deal with death as a normal part of life. So when death comes unexpectedly or violently, our resources are totally inadequate. Denial has become our automatic but inadequate response.

Stage-Two Shock: Numbness

Once the information is heard, survivors go into a second stage of shock in the form of numbness. Here people fear painful, overwhelming, and monstrous feelings, and they try to keep these emotions at bay.

When people are in self-protective denial or anesthetic numbness, it doesn't help to ask how they feel, because they do not feel anything.

Listen to Their Story

What can we say? Out of the fear of saying the wrong thing, many of us avoid reaching out to survivors. This is our greatest failure, because it is not what we say but our quiet presence and our nonjudgmental listening that mean the most to people in pain.

Listening to the story requires that we face some of our own fears. We may fear that what happened to others will happen to us. We know better, but at some superstitious level we wonder, *Maybe it's contagious*. It is upsetting to speak of danger and death, but life's losses and limits await each of us. Listening won't affect the odds or the time of these events, but it will help us to better understand our reactions and appreciate our lives while we offer a hand to survivors.

One of the dead teen's neighbors mourned, "He always said 'Hi' to me, I always said 'Hi' to him. I never thought anything like this would happen. It could happen to any of our kids."

Most of the time our mission is to close our mouths, open our minds, and allow the person to speak the unspeakable. For those unable to voice what has happened, when we gently ask the who, what, when, where, and how questions, we can sit with them, hear the news, and accept their silent grief.

. . . Over and Over Again

The number of times the information must be heard to be processed is proportionate to the magnitude of the crisis. When we talk of our immediate and greatest losses, we repeat ourselves. This helps us to hear the unhearable.

When children mourn the death of important people in their lives, they take longer than adults. Children may go down like submarines with their unspoken grief. Or chatter nonstop just to fill uncomfortable silences. As with adults we need to ask them if they want to talk about it. Calmly restating and reflecting their anger, sadness, and confusion helps them to overcome their fears of these downside emotions. On the upside, before we start sharing our loving memories of the dead we need to ask children whether they want to hear them. Suggesting that teens keep a diary of their chaotic emotions may also be helpful.

If we bring children to see a survivor, they will also ask what to say and do. One of our sons, age nine at the time, was about to visit his grandmother, whose brother had just died. In explaining what happened, we had carefully avoided saying that his great-uncle "went to sleep and never woke up" or "was taken to heaven." We didn't want to create fears of sleeping or God. When he asked what to say, his mother told him, "Just say, 'I'm sorry.'" His response? "But I didn't do it."

What could we tell him? There are no magic words. Nothing will bring back the dead, and guilt or denial is seldom productive for long. Sharing the sorrow is all we can do—and everything that we can do emotionally. When we say "I'm sorry," it means, "I'm sorry this happened to you."

Offer Practical Help

When others are in shock, we can help with both extraordinary and everyday tasks. The survivor in shock may seem like a broken robot. Crises disorganize, drain, and disorient. We can bring quarters for the hospital phone, make fresh coffee, feed the dog, answer the doorbell, put sympathy cards or flower tags in a box, do dishes, provide child care, help select a cemetery plot or headstone or clothes for the funeral services, mow the lawn, vacuum, notify the newspapers the dead person read or the groups to which he or she belonged, do laundry, bring dinner, and do anything they might request that we are willing to do. Rather than asking the survivors to figure out their needs and to choose an appropriate task for us, it is better to see what needs to be done and ask if we can do it.

Wouldn't the parents of the dead teens want "only family" in the days following the robbery? Wouldn't other people just be in the way? Wouldn't the parents be ashamed and want to be by themselves? Such worries often keep us away, but visits from friends help the parents feel that they are still accepted by the community. Consoling friends bring some warmth and light to the dark emptiness. We need to go, we need to call, and we need to write.

When we send a sympathy note, we are free to express our feelings in the strongest language. To a survivor our words will only begin to describe the pain. Our recollections of special times spent with people who die attest to their importance to us while alive and their continued influence on us through memory.

People entering hospitals or nursing homes appreciate picture albums, tapes, and rides outside. Often when an illness is a long one, the attention comes only at the beginning or at the end. One thoughtful visitor wrote a "news" letter, made copies and mailed them to everyone who had sent earlier good wishes. The letter brought a sack of cards and notes to a lonely friend who was beginning to feel forgotten.

Ram Dass and Paul Gorman write about these gifts in *How Can I Help?*: "There's more to the deed than the doer and what's been done. You yourself feel transformed and connected to a deeper sense of identity ... with the all-inclusive immensity of the universe."

Share Your Time, but Not Your Story

Nina Herrmann Donnelley, a chaplain, writes movingly and knowingly in *I Never Know What to Say*. What were her needs when she called friends after a man she had dated for a year and a half died suddenly of a massive heart attack? "Once they were on the phone ... they became ears for my voice ... and that, at the time, was all of me." She goes on to explain that in the acute state of bereavement only the self exists.

When we talk with survivors, we are there to hear what happened to them. People in shock have a hard time just coming to terms with their story and they cannot listen to ours, no matter how similar. We can best use our experience as survivors to know how important it is just to listen. In the next chapter we will explore how to patiently and compassionately support survivors as they struggle to accept the unacceptable and reluctantly return to living.

25

It's a Long Road
Back to Living

*"We begin by imagining that we are giving to them;
we end by realizing that they have enriched us."*
—POPE JOHN PAUL II

After Gracie Allen died in late August 1964, George Burns went into a deep depression for many years. For a long time, although he knew that she was gone, he still looked for her everywhere he went. He was devastated by the loss and could not imagine building a new existence without Gracie. Sleep was a major problem. First he had trouble falling asleep, then he would wake during the night, expecting her to be there beside him.

In *Living It Up* George describes his first good night's rest after Gracie's death. On an impulse he had climbed into her bed rather than his own. Maybe he was able to sleep restfully because he finally felt physically close to her presence for the first time in months. He wrote that this was "the beginning of the end of my deep mourning period."

Slowly, over time, George began going out to dinner with

friends and then, when he was ready, resumed work. Still making at least two professional appearances a month, on his ninety-seventh birthday he quipped that he didn't feel any older than the day before, when he was only ninety-six. He continues to dazzle audiences around the world with his joyful energy and love of life.

They Are Not Ready to Hear It

As the weeks pass and we continue to make ourselves available to people who have suffered grievous losses, we may find their fear, guilt, and anger to be overwhelming. As a result we may try to reassure the person and ourselves in premature and unhelpful ways. Because each experience in life teaches us, it is tempting to share our stories and the lessons we may have learned. But life's lessons are presented for independent study. If we are going to learn them, each of us has to do that at our own pace and for ourselves.

The overused phrases below were collected from survivors who reported how upsetting and useless they found the words when they were in crises. Some of the ways that these clichés backfire follow each group of phrases:

"At least you know your son's struggles are over."
"It's probably for the best."
"It could be a lot worse."
"She had a full life."
"She's better off now."

Even if these statements are true, they minimize and trivialize the survivor's pain. They don't take away from the person's loss and may subtly imply that he or she should feel guilty for wanting the lost one back.

"Don't talk like that. You'll lick this thing in no time."
"Don't take it so hard."
"Hold back your tears, you're upsetting people."
"When are you going to get back to work?"
"Why don't you just snap out of it?"

These are very critical statements and suggestions. They suggest inadequacy and undermine the person's competence. If the person could snap out of it or get back to work, they would. These phrases suggest the person intends to remain stuck. They are subtle put-downs and imply that the person is not coping well.

The frustration and impatience of these phrases are usually the result of ignorance. We may not know that grief often takes years instead of weeks or months. Social pressure to race through mourning can be cruel. Too often we discourage those who are dying from raging against death. We also tend to discourage those who are grieving from taking time to adjust to their losses.

Other Responses That Don't Help

When one of our two most important boundaries, our homes or our bodies, is violated, it threatens our basic sense of security and creates long-lasting effects.

"Why don't you live in a safer neighborhood?"
"What were you doing out so late at night?"

These blame the victim and question his or her judgment in a parental way.

"I know how you feel."

This is nearly impossible, denies the person's uniqueness, and usually provokes an angry spoken or unspoken "No, you don't."

"Things will get better. Everything will be all right."
"It'll be okay."
"You'll get over it."

These imply you've found a crystal ball that can predict the future.

"Aw, don't be so unhappy, look on the bright side."
"Why don't you take something for your nerves?"
"Don't you want me to call your doctor?"

These are condescending and suggest that we only want to hear about good things and that we may not be there for them unless they cheer up or take some drugs.

"I know you feel disappointed, but there's always another time."

This implies we can read a person's body language perfectly and we want them to feel a different feeling.

"I can see you're upset/sad. That makes me upset/ sad too."

This may be more accurate information than other phrases, but suggests that the person has made us upset. This can burden them with our needs or lead them to feel guilty for becoming upset.

When we use these phrases, we do so with the best of intentions. It may be better to be there and say the wrong thing than to avoid people in pain and leave them alone with their misery. The sheer number of these clichés show how desperately we all want to find some comforting words.

The word *crisis* may be overused in politics and the media, but our insensitivity to people who survive rape and robbery can victimize and isolate the victim almost as much as the crimes themselves.

What *should* we do for the victims? We can treat them as if they were physically wounded, assist in practical ways, and help them to stop blaming themselves.

Time Takes Time

The results of the first studies of marital couples before *and* after a spouse dies, conducted by Camille Wortman, of the State University of New York, and colleagues in California and Michigan, surprised the researchers. Life-satisfaction scores did not match the scores of those who hadn't lost a spouse for an average of ten years. It took twenty years for their depression scores to return to the same level.

Many of us expect too rapid a recovery. Until now conventional wisdom held that a year or two would suffice. Even so, we recently learned of a woman whose husband asked her, "What's wrong?" just three weeks after her father had died.

One of us received a long-distance phone call at three-thirty A.M., from a friend in another city whose father had died. Our friend's mother was in such a state of shock that she wouldn't leave his body. By talking with us over the phone, our friend came to realize that he wanted someone to fix the unfixable. He seemed to appreciate our listening to him. Once we had heard his pain, he was able to listen and respect his mother's need to stop the clock, at least for a little longer.

For some, healing takes a lifetime. More than thirty years after her death George Burns still refers in every performance to his life with Gracie. After a child dies, 70 percent of marriages fail. The partners are just too needy. The parents of the two teens who died in the robbery above are facing a long road back. The best solution is often to seek professional help from the beginning to guide them through the daily process of the talking, the listening, the accepting, the remembering, and the putting aside.

Feeling Stoppers

There are no one-liners, simple solutions, or special ways of instantly lifting grief or removing fear. There are none because the need is not to stop the feelings but to hear and accept them.

Why do we want to stop someone else's feelings? The feelings of grief, rage, and despair are intense. It is hard to be in touch with such powerful emotions because they may remind us of our own crises and our own uncontrollable feelings. Maybe they are like the feelings that overwhelmed us in the past. Maybe they are like the ones we most fear experiencing in the future.

When we try to stop these emotions and look for an easier road, we not only find a dead end but we communicate a frightening message. We tell our fellow sufferers that the feelings on the journey are too intense for us and that they will have to go it alone.

Unfortunately these one-line phrases cut off feelings just when a person needs to feel deeply. In addition they carry a hidden criticism: "There is something wrong with you." It's as if we want to talk people out of their pain or perceptions so that they'll have the "right" ones. This won't work. Since there are no right feelings to be had, it brings on feelings of inadequacy. These pat sayings separate us and undermine our confidence, rather than connecting us and supporting our fellow travelers.

When we don't know what to say, we can tap the power of touch. We can hold their hand, stroke their brow, and smooth their hair. This is especially true when people feel sick, alone, and untouchable.

Knowing Your Personal History of Loss

How can we become more comfortable with intense feelings? There are several ways. One of the best is to change the way we think about them. In earlier chapters of this book, we have emphasized how important it is for the stressed-out person to experience his or her emotions in all their intensity, and to label them. It is equally important to review our own past traumas to see where we may be vulnerable to overreacting and to stopping other people's emotions. In this way our supportive interaction with others can help us to become aware of our own unresolved conflicts and to heal our old wounds.

If someone is the victim of a crime, for example, and we were abused as a child, that person's helplessness and pain may remind us of our own experience and may overwhelm us. This is not to say that we have to avoid supporting people in these situations. In helping others deal with their grief, we can often help ourselves with our grief.

If we are aware of the connection, we will be better prepared to handle the feelings as they emerge. We may also need to find a way to make sense out of the incidents. In order to get beyond the experience, we have to remember, accept, and forgive.

Staying in touch with our personal histories as we support others can defend us from overreacting to the losses of life that may be most upsetting for us. Reviewing our loss history may also help us to recognize that there are issues that we cannot resolve on our own. Sometime it is wise to share the burden of supporting people going through particular types of crises that we are not yet equipped to handle.

Fortunately there are school counselors and crisis-intervention teams. In the case of the teens who died, the president of the school board announced that their crisis team would be activated the next morning to help students deal with the event. As she said, "This will hit very, very hard."

If survivors are withdrawing and are not yet hooked up to help, it is often very important to seek them out. Sometimes we want to be alone with our pain or our dying. Many animals instinctively nurse their physical wounds alone or leave the pack to die. Often the terminally ill die in the early-morning hours or wait until everyone is out of their hospital room before they die. Sometimes we need to let go. Not being there can also be a gift.

The wishes of those in distress must be respected. At times, however, their withdrawal sets up a vicious cycle. As they begin avoiding us, we begin avoiding them. Some of us do so out of respect, others do so because they feel rejected. This isolation may lead to inactivity or resignation and it may deepen a depression, as the person finds life increasingly lonely and empty.

Recovery

The patterns of grief are many. Money, position, intelligence, and self-confidence do not protect people from distress when a loved one dies.

The largest study to look at these variables over time was mentioned earlier. Researchers interviewed 2,867 people before and 92 after the loss of a spouse. The greater the person's income, intelligence, and self-esteem, the more depressed the person became after the loss. Young white males took longer to recover than blacks and the elderly.

What makes the biggest difference? Even support from friends and family may not be the buffers once thought. In these studies one's social network had very little, if any, effect. Does this mean that supporting survivors is wasted effort? We don't believe so.

Apparently those with greater resources may view the world as more controllable, predictable, and secure than those with less. Uncontrollable events may hit these people harder because the events shatter their worldview. Crises undermine everyone's sense of control. Unfortunately only 20 to 30 percent of survivors are able to make sense of the loss. Studies also find that survivors who are unable to find meaning soon after the loss are unlikely to find it years later.

What can we do to help? Should we offer a new worldview? People often try to do this by sharing their beliefs, such as:

"This is God's will."
"We have no right to question God."
"God must have had a good reason for taking her."
"God must love you or he wouldn't give you this burden."
"When God closes a door, he opens a window."

Is this the best time to preach? People need holding, not scolding. Faith is a source of strength for some, but others question their faith in a crisis. We best leave spiritual counseling to the Spirit or the clergy.

These religious-sounding statements also ask survivors to disguise or deny their feelings in dangerous ways. It's as if we are telling them that they will receive support only if they conceal how they actually feel. On the other hand, validating their feelings is supportive. If a Christian, for example, is struggling with anger and feeling guilty about it, it may help to remind him that even Jesus questioned God angrily from the cross, saying, "My God, my God, why hast thou forsaken me?" Suppressed rage about a meaningless tragedy will only smolder and haunt them later.

When survivors ask, "Why me?" "Why did God do this to me?" "Why is he dying?" along with the many other forms of these questions, they are not asking us for answers. They do so to confront the crisis and their worldview. It is best to remain silent or to admit that we do not know.

Perhaps the best we can do is to allow the bereaved the space to struggle with these questions and believe in their ability to find answers for themselves. We can assure them with our presence that we will be there to share their grief and that we will not abandon them when they need us most. Beyond this, each of us must silently seek comfort from our own worldview in order to comfort others.

Check in Consistently Without Making Demands

Grief is a long, lonely journey. Sharing that openly with a survivor can be a turning point. In addition it can remind us that even if our help is not necessary at one bend in the road, we need not feel rejected. We can keep checking in on the survivor's progress. We can make frequent, brief visits. At some difficult passage we may be the only one there to lean on.

It helps to continue discussing everyday events and concerns. Many parents whose children have died find that people don't know how to deal with shared memories after the tragedy. Most parents want us to bring up their dead children in conversation and enjoy talking about them as much or more than other parents.

It is important to keep planning pleasant, time-limited events and inviting the survivor. A dinner with friends, a Sunday ride in the country, or a funny movie can gently bring people back to living and lift feelings of sadness. We can also ask the survivor, "What things have helped you the most?"

If we find ourselves unappreciated, it usually reflects the survivor's necessary self-centeredness. We can make a log for ourselves of our efforts in order to help us know that we made a difference.

If the crisis involves a career or financial setback, we may want to lend the person money. Giving of ourselves is usually far more important than giving of our possessions. Nonetheless sometimes the need is great and we are in a position to help. In these cases it may be better to give than to lend. As the saying goes, it often costs about the same. In addition we may lose a friend who cannot face us without returning the money or may resent the burden when the loan is repaid. One of the best ways to give money is to ask the person to repay us by giving it to still another person they find in need and asking that person to do the same.

Let's Allow Them to Do Us a Favor

Toward the end of the journey it may help to make some small requests or demands to offer the survivor a chance to resume the give-and-take of the relationship. Baby-sitting, carpooling children, or other tasks that involve taking care of us or those we love can help them feel less indebted. When they feel that they have mastered the situation, regained their connections, and returned their self-esteem to normal levels, the healing process is well on its way.

The next chapter, about preventing burnout, is required reading. Required? Yes, because unless we take care of ourselves, we can't take care of others.

26

Preventing Burnout

We can't control or be responsible for others; we can only offer help in responsible ways.

On edge and restless for weeks, Joyce, a thirty-four-year-old homemaker, felt vaguely unsettled. Mark, her husband, was turning forty. When she answered the phone in the morning and heard his voice, Joyce knew something was wrong. Mark explained that he'd been turned down for the promotion. Convinced that he would never become a vice president, he sounded depressed.

At first Joyce welcomed the opportunity to help Mark. It made her feel needed. As he became more withdrawn and despondent, however, Joyce tried even more desperately to cheer him up. She spent more time at home with Mark and gradually dropped out of aerobics, church, and other activities. Soon Joyce started to feel like a failure. She grew angry over his unresponsiveness and worried that he had stopped loving her.

Knowing Our Limits

Joyce was suffering the early-warning signs of burnout. What can we learn from this overused word? Burnout means to be burning with desire and dedication only to find that our flame is dying out from exhaustion and frustration. Burnout is most common among the teachers, nurses, parents, and other helping occupations. It takes place gradually, as we give more and more of our limited resources in the hopes of helping but receive fewer and fewer results and rewards.

Joyce's problem was not new. As an adviser to her friends she often found herself drowning in their troubles. Even earlier, when Joyce was growing up, she played family peacemaker and kept her younger siblings from annoying her hardworking mother. When Joyce helped others, she felt strong, useful, and important.

The anger and fear Joyce now experienced, however, erupted from unmet needs and unrealized expectations. Instead of feeling competent and connected, Joyce felt drained, useless, and unloved. Instead of making a big difference in the way Mark handled his loss, Joyce felt she wasn't making any difference at all. Not only that, she felt that she had given up her friends and interests to no avail.

In trying to be Mark's support system Joyce thought she was entering a sprint instead of a marathon. Most major crises, including Mark's mid-life setback, however, take time to resolve because they call for developing new meanings and resolving our very purpose in living. Crises demand remapping our lives. Since most of us resist radical change, we tend to wallow in our losses for a time before we can acknowledge the need for change.

This may be why Mark seemed so stubbornly unresponsive. Perhaps he was letting his old goals die and needed to mourn them before he could make room for new goals. We cannot change before we are ready to change. Helpers need to know and accept this, or they risk burnout.

Why Limits Liberate Everyone

Without limits we not only set ourselves up for burnout, we also undermine the other person's self-confidence. The longer we talk about the problem, the larger it looms and the more it seems to defy solution or accommodation. In addition, if we gather too much intimate information from people, we may alienate and isolate them later on, when they are embarrassed by what they shared. Over time the amount of support given yields diminishing benefits at increasing costs to everyone.

By keeping our interactions short, we support people's self-esteem and reassure them that we will have energy and time when they need more of our help. Limits make it possible to support everyone's competence and connectedness. True support helps people solve their own problems rather than giving them a solution. It enables people to be their own counsel, be true to their own intuition, and follow their own best advice.

If we begin to overdo, go beyond support, and take responsibility for the other's sense of well-being, we put ourselves at risk of going on tilt or burning out. As we've said earlier, if we don't take care of ourselves, we can't take care of anyone else.

We need to recognize our limits and monitor our reserves. There comes a time when our resources are so depleted that we begin operating less effectively and put ourselves and others at risk. If we keep putting other people's needs above our own, we create a lose-lose situation.

When this begins to happen, we need to gently question our motives. Are we trying to win love, control another person, or alleviate our own stress by helping? Once we clarify the need, chances are good that we can fill it in more productive ways.

By setting limits clearly, honestly, and firmly we can free ourselves so that we can be fully there when others need us most. If limits are difficult to set, we may have invested too much in our single solution, rather than allowing others to explore their options and think about their choices.

There Are Always Options

To avoid the seductive snare of the single solution, it helps to remember that whatever situation anyone faces, there are many options. First, we can leave the scene or get rid of the problem at a well-chosen time. Second, we can learn to live with or accept the problem by getting our needs met in other ways. Third, we can change all or some part of the problem. Fourth, we can let time take its course or see if the problem itself changes. Finally, we can reframe or reinterpret the problem as a solution by finding something beneficial about it.

The last option is often overlooked and deserves to be clarified by example. The Little League baseball player was learning the power of positive thinking. Each time he tossed the ball in the air and tried to hit it, he would tell himself, *I'm the greatest baseball player in the world.* After hundreds of strikes and before he could get more instruction, he stopped and said, *I'm the best pitcher in the world.* Now, that's reframing!

Letting Go

We not only need to stop looking for the one right solution and expecting others to use it, we also need to let go of responsibility for things we cannot control. This includes everything from what happens in people's lives to how they handle it. Each response people make to the questions we ask in H.E.L.P. and H.E.A.L.T.H.Y. is their responsibility, not ours. Given their situation, they will do the best they can.

Growing up, we are told repeatedly, "You need to take more responsibility" and "Be responsible." Like the Puritan ethic of "Work is good," no one ever tells you *how much* work or responsibility is good.

Let's start with what happened. When life deals anyone bitter blows, they may withdraw, freeze, or strike out. If we forget to "agree-or-set-free," we may strike back or make demands or feel guilty because it happened to them and not us.

Guilt is a nearly useless emotion with its underlying assault on self-worth, but even regret implies that we are very powerful and caused the event.

We are not as powerful as we think. We don't control much, and often even that control is an illusion. By disputing our irrational beliefs about our control and responsibility, we can get back on our feet, provide support, and feel more in control of ourselves.

We are also not responsible for other people's feelings and thoughts. When it comes to the *E* in H.E.L.P. and the *E*, *A*, and *T* in H.E.A.L.T.H.Y., it's important to remember that people's reactions are not based on what is actually happening but on their perception and interpretation of what's happening. Their understanding is based on their previous experience in similar situations, the story they created about that experience, and the likelihood that it will be repeated.

We have no way of undoing the past, and there is usually little we can do to change the here-and-now except to control our own behavior. By not taking responsibility for other people's thoughts and emotions, we will have a much easier time hearing their pain, anger, and confusion. We will also have a much easier time responding to their ideas and feelings. Rather than reacting defensively, we can respond in supportive ways. This allows them room to adjust the ways they think and feel and to solve their problems in whatever way is comfortable for them, when they are ready to do so.

The Messenger Is Not Responsible for the Mess

Sometimes as the bearer of bad tidings we are blamed because people forget to separate the messenger from the message. When this happens, we can avoid counterattacking by first acknowledging people's unhappiness and the appropriateness of their reaction given the circumstances. It gives them permission to feel what they feel. We can encourage them to think about a plan to solve the problem or handle the feelings. By working on this together, we can also feel better about our relationship and we can communicate that feeling by saying yes to what others experience.

Not taking responsibility for things we cannot control relieves us of the obligation to fix things or feelings. We can give others room to solve their problems in their own way and in their own time. If Mark chooses to withdraw, sulk, and even refuse to talk about his disappointment, Joyce needn't feel hurt. Recognizing that it's not her responsibility, she can let Mark get back in control of his thoughts, feelings, and actions.

When we extend ourselves too far out on a limb or lean over backward to reach someone, we risk falling and getting hurt. By standing squarely on both feet and keeping our own balance, we provide stability for the person we are helping. We can certainly reach out our hand to steady the other person or offer our shoulder to lean against, but we cannot allow someone to push us on tilt.

Giving Rather Than Paying

When we give freely because we have resources to spare, giving is a pleasure and makes us feel good. There is a sense of joy that fills us and allows us to keep giving. When we respond to demands that are above and beyond what we want to give, we feel a sense of depletion. This makes it harder to keep giving.

By setting limits early in the process, we allow our emotional batteries to recharge. Knowing that we can say no makes it possible to enjoy saying yes.

As soon as we feel that we are starting to burn out and there is still more that we want to do for someone else, we need to stop and ask ourselves if it is worth our personal cost. Will we resent the person later? Can we continue to give at this time without strings attached? If we don't stop and think, we may say or do something that we will later regret. We can't unstab a wound, and one cutting remark may leave a deep gash.

Relationships are too important to risk destroying them with a few poorly chosen words.

To prevent creating a new mess, we may need to ask people what they expect of us and how urgent and important the problem is to them. We may need to ask ourselves, *Who else could I recruit to help out? Is there any way I can turn this drudgery into fun?* and *Can I take some time out for myself and regain my strength before helping?*

If it's important and urgent, but we can't delegate or transform the work and we have to take care of ourselves, we need to let the other person know we care about her and that we wish it could be different. We must be clear that what we have to do for ourselves is very important to us. We must also be specific about what we can offer in the way of time and resources, and be prepared to accept her disappointment or anger. On the other hand, we may reassess the situation and decide to help. Knowing that we can say no may make saying yes less of a burden.

One of us applied these lessons when her son, Rob, asked for company and a second opinion in looking at a house that he was thinking of buying. The home was located at some distance in another township, and it was not only a beautiful spring day but it was a day already committed to overdue gardening chores. Rob accepted her decision not to accompany him and joined her in gardening.

Working together, they made great progress, and suddenly she decided that the ride would give her a chance to catch up on the details of his life and also to enjoy some sunlit scenery. Instead of being a burden that prevented her from doing what she wanted to do, the trip became an opportunity that she cherished. When our nos are expressed and accepted, it allows us to say yes freely.

Recommending Professional Help for Mental Illness

The goals of this book are limited and do not include the assessment of mental illness or its treatment. Occasionally we use H.E.L.P. or H.E.A.L.T.H.Y. and uncover a serious problem for which the person should seek professional help. There are many signs and symptoms we could list. Here are a few red flags to watch for, followed by a framework for helping others decide if they might need counseling.

When people are unable to work, play, or go to school because of substance abuse or changes in eating, sleeping, or relating, their problems may be serious. Watch out for excessive fears or panic episodes, severe depression or prolonged withdrawal, suicidal or homicidal thinking, extreme mood swings or confused thinking, and hearing or seeing things others don't hear or see. Any of these could be a cry for help.

Can we harm them by using H.E.L.P. or H.E.A.L.T.H.Y.? No. They may appear more upset for a short while because the interaction may bring their stress to the surface, but if we accept their emotions and help them sort through their options, they are likely to be helped.

Suicide Prevention

What about the suicidal person? Could we push the person over the edge by talking about it? No. As Edwin Shneidman, Ph.D., of UCLA's School of Medicine and a pioneer in suicide prevention, says, "Pain is what the suicidal people seek to escape. The immediate goal should be to reduce their pain in every way possible." Talking supportively, hearing their pain, acknowledging their suffering, and avoiding the temptation to falsely reassure or cheer them up can reduce their sense of isolation and worthlessness. Finding out how we can intervene with parents, teachers, spouses, or bosses on their behalf can also be of help.

The second major goal is to cut through their tunnel vision

that suicide is their only option. Suicide is a permanent solution to temporary problems. Broadening their perspective and their options can make the crucial difference. H.E.L.P. and H.E.A.L.T.H.Y. are lifelines if we don't panic and don't try to control their feelings or behavior.

What else can we do? There is a myth that those who talk about suicide don't commit it. If we can stay with the person and remove all means for suicide or arrange for the family to do so, we can make a difference. Rather than a betrayal of trust, if we can't persuade someone to seek professional help, it is an act of true friendship to contact and alert the person's family.

The most important thing we can do for someone struggling with a mental illness is to help the person get appropriate diagnosis and treatment. This may mean recommending professionals or facilities that we respect. It may mean offering to make an appointment and accompanying a person who is depressed to the doctor and then encouraging them to take medication if prescribed. Or it may mean offering to call a support group for grieving parents so that a volunteer will make the call that most people later regret not making sooner.

Recommending Counseling for a Crisis

What about those in crisis with no clear signs of mental illness? H.E.L.P. and H.E.A.L.T.H.Y. will go a long way, but one way to help people decide if they need counseling is to ask them how competent, connected, and active they feel they are. Those who are withdrawing and oversleeping or becoming frantically active but unproductive may need professional help, especially if they feel worthless and isolated. We can reassure them and ourselves that with time and counseling most people will improve and feel considerably better.

Often people will resist our suggestions. This does not mean we have failed. Remember, we are not responsible for the problem or the solution. If the situation does not turn out the way we had hoped, we must acknowledge that we did our best. It is time to accept our limitations, move on, and focus on how we can be helpful, given what is happening now. Perhaps we just have to leave it be.

The help we offer may be a fragile seed that may need to be nurtured slowly before it will flower. We must trust the process. We are not the sun or the water, we are only farmers with watering cans. Chungliang Al Huang, tai ji master, shares his wisdom:

> *"Sitting quietly,*
> *Doing nothing.*
> *Spring comes,*
> *The grass grows by itself."*

Staying Close but Out of the Way

All of this is even more important when we are helping a family member. Researchers are just beginning to discover how overinvolvement can be destructive. What are some of the drawbacks and pitfalls?

First, the intensity of our relationship may interfere with our ability to define the problems accurately. Second, we may focus too much on solutions or demonstrations of our helpfulness. This leaves the recipient feeling incompetent, guilty, and resentful. Third, our intrusiveness may backfire when the family member says, "Your suggestions don't work. Leave me alone already!"

While some families pull together in times of crisis, if the crisis is long-term, the recipients may feel that they have let the family down because they didn't get over their crisis. Sometimes we accuse the one in crisis of having the wrong attitude or we monitor him too closely and undermine his motivation. Saying, "No, I won't," even if it is self-defeating, may be the only way the person can regain control and self-respect.

By backing off and yet remaining available, the frequency of caring and loving interactions can be increased and the relationship can become stronger and more satisfying.

Retracing Our Steps

In this book we've looked at ways to better understand how we all fight-flee-or-freeze under stress and how the domino effect disrupts our lives. We've seen how we can take our own pulse when attacked by people who are stressed-out and disarm others by agreeing or setting them free.

Through H.E.L.P. and H.E.A.L.T.H.Y. ways, we've found how to offer social support and create a more caring world around us. We've also connected in physical as well as emotional ways that soothe and offer first aid for stress without undermining people's sense of competence. Finally, by meeting our own needs when stressed-out and accepting our limitations, we can avoid burnout, even in the most tragic of situations.

Epilogue

You've got the tools now. How you use them is up to you. We've found H.E.L.P.ing stressed-out people to be highly rewarding. We hope that you will share this experience.

Perhaps the very next time you spot someone in a fight-or-flight-or-freeze situation, you will feel competent to offer H.E.L.P. and Support. We hope that in all of your relationships you will be able to agree, set free, or connect with people in a variety of empowering ways.

It has been said that "as a species, we often take the best approach only after we have tried all the others." Perhaps that's true, but as individuals we can make choices about how we respond to one another's stress and confusion. Our living places at home, at work, and at play can be filled with light and joy or darkness and loneliness. We can create warmth or we can wait to see how cold it becomes.

There is no need to sulk in a corner and complain about a

lack of community. We know how to build communities. We can come together and celebrate our diversity. Let's connect.

Stressed-out or not, let's make each person feel competent and valued. With this kind of support, each of us can rejoice in the challenge of an ever-changing world without going on tilt.

We have the tools, we have the will, the choice is ours. Together we can build the caring community that we all want and need.

Now That We've Connected, Don't Be a Stranger

This can be the beginning rather than the end of our relationship. Please share your experiences with stressed-out people and your H.E.L.P. and H.E.A.L.T.H.Y. stories by writing us. Our publisher will forward your letters. The address is:

Ronald Nathan and Marian Stuart
c/o Ballantine Books
201 East 50th Street
New York, New York 10022

Hearing from you would bring us joy.

Index

RONALD G. NATHAN, PH.D., is a practicing clinical psychologist and professor in the Departments of Family Practice and Psychiatry of Albany Medical College. He is the coauthor of a number of books, including *Stress Management: A Comprehensive Guide to Wellness* and *The Doctors' Guide to Instant Stress Relief*. An award-winning teacher, Dr. Nathan developed and evaluated the country's first required stress management course for medical students. He has conducted stress management workshops for groups as diverse as homemakers, police officers, accountants, teachers, nurses, lawyers, secretaries, and dentists. Dr. Nathan has also lectured and consulted for numerous firms, including Merrill Lynch, Blue Cross, ERA Real Estate, and AT&T.

MARIAN R. STUART, PH.D., is a clinical associate professor and Director of Behavioral Science in the Department of Family Medicine at the University of Medicine and Dentistry of New Jersey, Robert Wood Johnson Medical School, and also holds an appointment in the Department of Psychiatry. She is the principal author of the highly successful textbook, *The Fifteen Minute Hour: Applied Psychotherapy for the Primary Care Physician* (Praeger Press, 1986; 2nd Ed., 1993). Dr. Stuart received her bachelor's degree in psychology, summa cum laude, from Kean College in 1971. She received her M.S. in 1973 and her Ph.D. in social/personality psychology in 1975, both from Rutgers University. The mother of three grown children, Dr. Stuart maintains a small private practice as a clinical psychologist in Morristown, New Jersey. She also lectures widely and presents workshops in areas of stress management, communications skills, geriatrics, family dynamics, and medical education.